LOCO'S, MEN and STEAM MEMORIES

Cyril Birchall

Oxford Publishing Company

ISBN 0-86093-316-4

Typesetting by:
Aquarius Typesetting Services, New Milton, Hants.

Printed in Great Britain by:
Biddles Ltd., Guildford and Kings Lynn

Published by:
Oxford Publishing Co.
Link House
West Street
POOLE, Dorset

British Library Cataloguing in Publication Data
Birchall, Cyril
    Locos, men and steam. — (Reminiscences)
    1. Locomotives — England — History
    I. Title II. Series
    625.2′61′0924   TJ603.4.G7

Acknowledgements

My thanks go to Rex Kennedy for his research in obtaining relative photographic material for this book of reminiscences, and for writing the captions, and also to Roy Anderson for providing much of the material for the book.

Contents

ILLUSTRATIONS

Between pages 32 and 33

Between pages 64 and 65

CHAPTER ONE

Telephone Attendant

In the summer of 1939, I sat an examination for the position of apprentice electrical engineer which I passed with flying colours, along with another boy of the same age, but as this boy's father was a VIP for the firm in question he was the one chosen by the powers that be. I have no bitterness about this, and the only reason I make this reference is to say that the successful applicant was to have taken up his apprenticeship on the first day of the forthcoming new year, when this particular company took on new apprentices.

I had earlier had my name taken for a possible vacancy on the London Midland & Scottish Railway and was delighted, a few weeks after this written test in which I did so well, when I received a letter requesting me to go to Chester for a medical examination, along with a free train ticket. I duly passed my medical and, ironically, started at Dallam Shed on New Year's Day 1940. Was it coincidence, luck or was it destiny? Who knows, but the fact was that, at 8a.m. on Monday, 1st January 1940 I, along with three other youths my age, were waiting outside the office at the bottom of the shed to be detailed for our new job.

Perhaps because I was the smallest of the quartet I was ushered to the foreman's lodge, generally known, as I learned later, as the 'hut', and there I was put under the jurisdiction of a youth about a year older than myself. His name was Wilf, and he was to show me the ropes as it were. My main duty was to issue time cards to drivers and firemen as they booked on for footplate duties; after they had written their time on the card I simply replaced it in the box-like container which housed the cards in numerical order. At the same time I was to give them a sponge cloth, for the purpose of keeping their hands free from dirt and oil, but as it was a time of austerity, I was to wait until they asked for one.

Men would also come to the the stores for oil, and it was my job to issue this. The oil, of which there were four kinds, was kept in tanks with a letter in white paint on the tank to denote the type. The one on the extreme left was marked with a 'T' and contained 'G' oil while the next one, which contained paraffin, had a large 'Q' clearly marked. Next to this was a tank with the letters 'BL', this also holding 'G' oil. Then, to complete the row, the one on the right was one with the letter 'H' prominently displayed, under which was a gas ring that was perpetually kept burning. This tank housed the black oil, a thick and slow running substance which necessitated the use of the constantly burning gas jet to keep it warm, otherwise it would never flow.

So, I mused, if one simply ignored the letters on each tank it would be easy to remember what they held. Wilf explained all this with a bit of a wry grin, and I smiled back with the acceptance of the comical situation. The door to the stores was a kind of counter which was hinged, and could be lifted to gain access or departure. Above this was a large gaping hole in the wall, so it can easily be imagined what it was like when cold winds rattled down the shed and smoke from the freshly-lighted locomotive fires cascaded into the stores. In addition to serving oil at this flap-cum-counter, I was to issue buckets holding spanners and detonators as well as shovels and buffer lamps. This was, of course, when we had such things in stock, which quite often we did not.

Between the oil stores and the foreman's hut was a wall, which spanned half-way across the width of the building, and was the medium of a chimney-breast which had two fires, one facing into the stores area and the other throwing heat into the foreman's half of the ramshackle enclosure. Round the whitewashed hearths of both fires was a piece of rail, the kind trains run on, bent in the shape of a three-sided 'oblong' and rubbed to a gleaming silver. Wilf told me it was my job to keep these fires stoked, the hearths whitewashed and the bent rail emery-papered.

Near the fire, which was in the foreman's half, was a desk about the height of a man's chest, this being from where the running of the shed was conducted by the Running Shift Foreman, to give him his correct title. He sat on a stool which was about a yard high, and although the reason for such a high stool was obvious, to reach the desk, the reason why the desk was so tall in the first place remained forever a mystery.

On the wall behind the Foreman's desk were four telephones, three being long, slender wooden box-like ornaments, while the fourth, on the right of these, was a smaller square-shaped instrument a foot or so higher than the rest. This was the exchange phone, and when my tutor informed me I was to answer these phones when they rang I found I had difficulty trying to speak into the mouthpiece, due to my lack of height. So it was arranged for a box to be made for me to stand on, this task being duly assigned to a grizzly-looking old codger known as Father Leopold, who resembled Father Time without his scythe. This ancient character was known to the shed staff as the 'Rough Carpenter', and anyone who used the handicraft he produced immediately appreciated the implication of the nickname.

I was to work three shifts, starting at 8a.m. days then afternoons starting at 4p.m. and a night shift which began at midnight, all of which lasted eight hours. The foremen, however, worked only two turns, afternoons and nights, so I would be with one foreman for two weeks then leave him on the third. Afterwards I would work with the other foreman for a further fortnight.

On the afternoon turn of my second week I was with Frank Heasom, a large-framed individual who was a singer in his time off-duty. He was an amiable person, and right from the start we got on extremely well, although I must confess he could be a bit of a tartar when anything upset him, and woe betide the poor unfortunate who caused him to lose his temper. Thankfully, I was never on the receiving end of his wrath. We soon became acquainted and he would often ask me the number of a particular driver (I knew their numbers off by heart after a short time) so that he would not waste time fingering through their route cards looking at their names, because as they were in numerical order it saved time to know their number. The foreman on the opposite shift was quite a different character. He was a man of diminished stature, quiet, and simply did his job with no fuss. His name was John Boucher, but I always called him 'Mister'.

After about three months I was promoted to cleaner, but as the war was some six months old and the country was fighting for survival I was retained on the same job, and apart from the fact that I received a rise in wages I was a cleaner in name only and, in fact, never did any cleaning at all.

A few weeks later, when I was working the midnight shift, I went to collect my wages, which were paid out on Fridays at noon. The boss asked me if I would like to 'pass out', and although I was not on duty I jumped at the chance so I, along with three other cleaners, went into the boss's office where a footplate inspector was waiting. The quartet which stood before him must have presented a comical sight, as the other three had just finished cleaning a dirty engine and were filthy to say the least, while I was smart and clean in my Sunday best. It was not a severe test, just the protection of trains, hand signals and a brief description of railway work in general, with a slight knowledge of the workings of a locomotive; this being mainly the passage of steam from the regulator valve to the cylinders and out to atmosphere. We had done some homework on these subjects, and the examiner was pleased with our efforts. Needless to say, we all passed.

I was overjoyed, but it was nothing like the thrill I had about a month later, just a few days after my seventeenth birthday, when I found my name on the enginemen's roster — I was a 'red ink' fireman. This term was used for cleaners passed for firing dutes, and who were marked for higher grade duties, for example firing. Similarly, passed fireman were also marked in red ink when performing driving duties, and when men became 'registered' they would then be marked in black ink.

CHAPTER TWO

My First Year's Firing

It was a beautiful Monday morning as I made my way to the shed to book on at 5.30p.m. for my very first firing turn. I felt on top of the world as I asked for my time card, then went to the engine board to ascertain the number of the locomotive we were to have on No. 15 shunt, the job we were marked to work.

The board was marked in order of scheduled departures from the depot, ours being 5-45; 15 SHUNT: 7652: 4; the number 4 indicating the road on which it was berthed. Our engine was an 0-6-0, commonly known as a standard shunt, and had been prepared by another set of men (engine crew) so this meant we were due off at 5.45a.m., 45 minutes being allowed when preparing one's own engine. Outside the shed I found No. 7652 and climbed aboard, depositing my personal belongings on the shelf above the bunker. On the screen plate above the firehole door I placed a bottle of cold tea, which would warm, slowly, and from which I could take a sip at any time. The practice of carrying cold tea in a bottle was generally accepted by the men throughout the system. It may be unhygenic and even replusive, but then it was taken as a matter of fact.

Standing on the little footplate, I thought what's the first thing I do, and realised, with a bit of a shock, that not only was I inexperienced but I was downright clueless. Fortunately Ozzy Tasker, a young fireman who had started his career as telephone attendant as I had, was on an engine on the next road to ours. He advised me to check my tools including the shovel, spanners, buffer lamps and so on which I did, not forgetting the fire-irons (dart, pricker and paddle), and I then used the dart to knock the fire round the firebox, feeling for clinker or rather the lack of it. I then replaced the dart safely on the side tank, and spread a round of coal on to the grate. This being done I placed the buffer lamps on the brackets, one at each end, and was ready to depart.

By this time my driver had arrived, bidding me a cheery good morning and telling me his name was George Allen, at the same time asking what was mine. I told him mine was Cyril Birch, and that this was my first turn as a fireman. He seemed an amiable person, not so tall, and smoked a pipe.

'Oh! You'll be all right' he laughed, and from this I understood that he was prepared to tell me anything I did not know, which, I mused, was quite a lot.

Assuring himself that we had everything we needed, he moved the engine towards the shed signal and asked me if I knew how to 'gong' off. When I said I did not know, he took me to the signal on which there was a little gong resembling that of a Morse code instrument. He then gave the gong a short sharp press, saying that that was a 'one', and upon receiving a 'one' back from the signalman he then gave 'two'. This, he explained, denoted that we wanted to travel towards Warrington Station, a 'three' being given for Froghall and 'four' for the direction of Winwick Quay, with a 'five' being given for Dallam Branch Sidings. The code of five was also given if an engine required to pass the signal in order to make a shunting movement, but this was rarely used as it wasted time, and the men on the shed shunting operations simply ignored it, and passed it at their own risk.

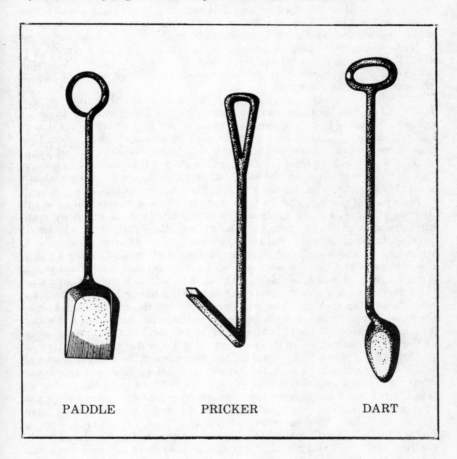

PADDLE   PRICKER   DART

On this occasion the signal was lowered without much delay, and George set off towards the stop block situated at the end of the engine line, adjacent to the main line. He brought the engine to a stand behind a square-shaped disc, white with a red horizontal band, and told me it was called a dummy. At length the dummy, with a violent jerk, turned a quarter clockwise, now sporting a red diagonal band. This was the 'clear' position, and we steamed gently across the 'down' slow, the 'down' fast, and on to the 'up' slow, the crossover road continuing into Dallam branch. Waiting a moment or two for the starting signal to be lowered, we set forth towards Froghall and then on to Warrington No. 2 box, past Warrington No. 1 box and then down a short incline, where we waited at the bottom to be called-on by the shunting staff. We had arrived.

After being called off the bank by a hand signal from the shunter, George backed our engine on to a long raft of wagons and told me to put a good fire on, as we would be required to drag this raft up a slight incline which was known as No. 2 neck. This was the neck we would be using on No. 15 shunt, while the engine which worked alongside us on the old side (so called because it was there long before the extension, the side we were on) was No. 14 shunt, and he would use No. 3 neck. On the east side of No. 3 neck was another one, shorter than the others and called No. 4 neck, the one on the west side being No. 1 neck.

Our job was simply to drag rafts up the neck, shunt them into various roads and then go back and come up again with another. From time to time I spread a round of fire on to the little grate of our locomotive as my driver bade me, topping up the boiler now and then by means of the injector. This was easier said than done, as the feed had to be manipulated until it 'sang' with no water leaking from the feedpipe. It did not take me long to master this as George showed me the knack, almost closing the feed when steam would blow and then quickly opening it to just the correct setting.

Time passed quickly, and then we were told by the shunter to have our 'twenty minutes', a slang expression meaning our food for which we were officially allowed twenty minutes. During the interval George, who loved yarning, began to tell me about his exploits in the Navy during World War I, when he was a stoker. I just sat there, taking it all in, and asking a polite question here and there — we were on friendly terms right from the off. After our meal it was necessary for the tank to be filled, so we went under the water-column where my mate handed up the heavy hose bag, which I placed along the tank for some way before putting the end into the hole in the tank. Then it was merely a matter of pulling the chain until the water was up to the top, but then I learned I had to wait until the water sank lower as the fact of the matter, in this case, was that the water took some time to go through the pipe which connected the two sides of the tank. It seemed I was learning quite a lot on this first day and before long, our relief was climbing up the handrails. We were due to be relieved at 12.35p.m., but as was the habit of most drivers they always came a few minutes before the appointed time. We were then allowed forty five minutes to walk from Arpley to Dallam Shed in order to book off, the driver being allowed a further ten minutes to make out his journals concerning his shift's work. George booked off at 1.30p.m., ten minutes later than me, so I bade him farewell and then made my way home, feeling happy.

Next morning came rather quickly, but I was up and preparing myself at the unearthly hour of 4.30a.m. On arrival at the shed I booked on duty, and ascertained the number of our engine from the board; we were marked to have No. 7376, again berthed on No. 4 road. Feeling a little more confident now, I spread the fire and checked our equipment, as Ozzy had instructed me the previous morning, and when George came I informed him we were ready to go. He gave me a complimentary smile, and told me to gong of.

That day was simply a repetition of the first, as indeed was the rest of the week. Thus it was when booking off on Saturday, with our week's work completed, that I must confess I was feeling the effects of six day's early rising. However, I had a free weekend ahead of me, as our next turn of duty began at 5.05p.m. the following Monday.

After a good rest over the weekend, I was at the shed on Monday evening to start my shift. On this duty we were diagrammed to prepare two big engines, an hour being allowed for each, and then walk to Arpley to relieve the men on No. 14 shunt at 7.50p.m. Under the supervision of my mate, and working as a team, we soon had them ready for the road. It was a dirty job carrying tools and oil, filling and trimming buffer lamps, so when this task was done we needed to wash our hands and generally clean up. Situated at the bottom of the shed was a cold water tap, an object shaped like a pillar-box except that it was much larger and whitewashed. This was where we carried out our ablutions, the water from this tap coming directly from the tank containing water from which the engines were filled and, needless to say, unfit for drinking. We simply turned on the tap and stood with feet apart to avoid splashing our legs, washing the grime off our hands under the pouring water.

As we now had some free time to ourselves we retired to the messroom. The door of the 'cabin', as it was referred to, opened to an antiquated latch operated by a heavy iron handle which, when pulled towards the would-be entrant, pushed a rod about a yard long upwards, lifting a square piece of metal on top of the door allowing it to open, falling back into place by its own weight when the door was closed. By the racket it made, it was impossible to enter without all the occupants knowing. Just beyond the door was a fire grate, generously heaped with hugh chunks of best Yorkshire coal which were burning heartily. To the side of this was a kettle the size of a barrel, which seemed destined to boil eternally.

Round the walls of the cabin was a sort of bench which continued right round the entire perimeter, resting on small balks of timber embedded into the walls about a yard apart which had obviously been implanted when the walls had been constructed. Two big tables, which were almost the full length of the one mantle gas-lit cabin, were solidly built of stout timbers that were white with continual scrubbing. It was in this place of repose that we spent the next half-hour, before setting off to Arpley where we arrived about ten minutes before the appointed time. Our engine was No. 12102, an ex-L&YR 0-6-0 tender engine known to all as a 'Lanky', on which an anti-glare sheet stretched from the top of the cab to the front of the tender, thus conforming to the black-out regulations. We climbed up the handrails and stood huddled together in a crouching position under the sheet, while the men being relieved struggled to put on their coats in the cramped space available. We waited for them to climb down before we attempted to take off our jackets and put them away.

There was a cupboard provided for our coats, but as this went right to footplate level it was difficult to open due to the fact that coal was always being squashed there by the action of the engine and footplate lap moving against each other. It was not a suitable place to store our food anyway, as the doors were anything but a flush fit, so most drivers put their food in the sand-box. The sand-boxes were positioned on each side of the footplate under the low sheeting, and had an iron lid which came clean off when lifted. Inside the boxes was a metal funnel down which sand was directed, by hand, straight on to the rail. The sand-box lid served as a seat, the only one available, and a piece of wood of any description, as long as it was flat and clean, was employed as a precaution against haemorrhoids.

In order to move the engine the driver was obliged to stand up, as the regulator handle was high above the boiler and he would have needed exceedingly long arms to operate it from a sitting position. The reversing wheel, located on the left-hand side, was made for strong-arm men as it required to be turned nineteen times from full-forward to full-reverse, so it can easily be imagined how the driver's arm was taxed to the full when shunting and reversing for a full shift. Due to the short cab, the man operating the regulator had to stand right up to the boiler front, dictated by the anti-glare sheet and, indeed, his stomach actually rested on the left-hand injector steam-valve, a wheel about 3in. across.

Unlike the standard shunt, which had a steam-brake, this class had a vaccum-brake which created the 21in. required by the small ejector which, when open, made a tremendous din. This type of brake was not brilliant, to say the least, because when it was slammed on after receiving a stop signal from the shunter, the wagons would drag us for two to three engine-lengths. Often this would cause the driver to reverse, as the wagons on the hump, where the shunter stood, would overrun the points, thus necessitating the driver to set back.

Firing this engine was no picnic for me either, because in order to put a round of fire on this type was little short of a contortionist act. The footplate was raised 6in. above the lap, so in order to shovel the coal I had to bend lower than my feet and then stand in a crouching position due to the sheet, an object which was the scornful recipient of many four-letter words. The narrowness of the footplate often caused the fireman to collide with the driver's backside, especially if he was reversing at that particular moment. Therefore I soon came to the conclusion, even with my limited experience, that the standard shunt was much more comfortable.

The 'Lanky's' injectors were a law unto themselves, and setting them to work was a masterpiece of skill even for the most experienced. The steam-valve was turned anticlockwise after slipping down the feed, about 6in. below, then manipulating it until it sang; in order to listen, one had to bring one's ear in close proximity to the feed, a precarious practice if the wagons snatched at that precise moment, as often happened. Very often the steam-valve wheels became obstinate and would only move under the forceful persuasion of the wheel spanner, a tool we rarely possessed due to acute shortage. We usually managed with any spanner.

Another curious trait with this kind of injector was that as the water in the tank became lower it would start to wobble, and often refused to work at all. George, my mate, showed me exactly what to do in that situation, as this happened when we had been shunting for an hour or so. He told me to fill the 'tallowpot' (a nickname given to the oilcan) with cold water from the tender, by means of a tap positioned about 6in. above the footplate lap. I was then to pour this water ever so carefully down the outside of the barrel of the injector, a treatment to which the reluctant apparatus usually responded, but not always. When it became apparent that it was not going to co-operate, it was necessary to take the feed handle out altogether, using a spanner, then pour the water down the inside of the barrel. This operation invariably did the trick, and happened at least once during a shift.

At 12.10a.m. we were relieved and began our long walk back to Dallam to book off at 1.05a.m., completing our eight hours. I then had the unpleasant task of walking home alone in the black-out, not a very palatable exploit for a lad of seventeen. That, however, was our work for the week, and Sunday morning came with a welcome.

The following week started with us booking on at the more humane time of 8.55a.m., this being a straightforward enough duty that simply involved walking to Froghall, relieving the warehouse shunt at 9.35a.m. and then working until 4.15p.m. when we would be relieved, allowing us to walk back to Dallam and book off at 4.55p.m. It was a grand morning as we stepped on to the standard shunt in the warehouse yard. This job was entirely different to the shunting on Arpley Sidings because here it was a matter of setting vans at precise points so that they could be unloaded, and then reloaded with goods for other places. As soon as we opened the regulator the shunter would give us a stop signal, even though we had moved only a matter of an inch or two, and after a while this became tedious — it was no wonder that most drivers hated this duty.

The sun came up determinedly and the day turned into a scorcher. I had recently been issued with overalls, the bib and brace kind, together with a jacket of the same material; being new they were hot, and coupled with the warm weather they became almost unbearable. Also the cab of a standard shunt went all over the footplate, and certainly did not help matters. George told me I could go and sit on the grass bank, which stretched along one side of the yard, but I thought I would be a coward if I capitualted so I stayed on the footplate. Fortunately, at 4.15p.m., I was relieved in both senses of the word. We worked this shunt from Monday to Friday, booking on at 5a.m. Saturday for the Dallam branch shunt. This made the week's work a good one, as far as the social aspect was concerned, for it meant we were on school hours with an early finish midday Saturday.

Shunting at Dallam was vastly different, as the yard here was surrounded by a number of industries including Walkers Brewery, the huge iron and steel mills of Dallam Forge, a foundry and a number of coal yards. The yard was virtually straight, with Dallam Lane running parallel along its full length, and it was a happy feeling to be close to people as they made their way up and down this busy thoroughfare. We could hear the tumultuous din of the rolling mills, see the girls in the brewery humping crates of beer, and watch the constant stream of men darting in and out of the two little public houses nestling cosily right in the middle of this hive of industrial activity.

Shortly after noon, the shunter said we were 'straight up', an expression used when the work was completed, and meaning that we could take her on the shed when we were ready. To do this we simply went to the top of the yard to a dummy, at the start of the crossover road which lead across the four main lines and on to the engine line. We then whistled 'three and a crow', a universal signal recognised anywhere to indicate that we wanted to cross the road. The dummy was eventually pulled off and we proceeded on to the stop block at the end of the engine line, moving forward from there on to an empty road on the depot. I then wound on the hand-brake, saw that the boiler was almost full, then collected the bucket of spanners and shovel and placed them in the stores. After booking off we parted and made our way home, the end of a perfect week.

All too soon it was Monday again, and we were booking on at 3.35p.m. This duty was the continuance of the shift the previous week, entailing a walk to the warehouse to relieve the previous duty at 4.15 p.m., this being where we would work until 10.55p.m. when we would be relieved. It was much cooler now, and quite pleasant to shunt along the main line. I had a close up view of the expresses as they stormed their way through Warrington, headed for the sharp rise to Acton Grange, and of the northbound trains which had just swept down this incline.

We did not use a great deal of steam on this duty, and the little bunker would easily last the 24 hours that the engine was away from the depot. At 6p.m. we backed on to a raft of vans to take them to Froghall Yard, which was on the other side of the main line. These vans were destined for the north, and indeed the yard was known as North End. After we had deposited these vans in the yard we went on to the loop in order to fill our little tank, there being no water-column on the warehouse side, with the one water-column serving both engines, and also train engines when necessary. As dusk approached I took the buffer lamps from the brackets, brought them on to the footplate and lit them in readiness for the dark hours.

Saturday saw us on the North End shunt as the warehouse was closed for the weekend, and with no sign of life across the road it seemed rather lonely at Froghall. The yard was flat, with no hump or gradient as at Arpley Sidings. We would drag a raft outside on to the 'down' loop, then the shunter would give us a robust 'hit 'em up' signal and my mate would give her plenty of regulator, sending the hooked-off shunts hurtling down the yard. When we were stopped by the shunter's arm being raised aloft, we would slam the brake on hard, then, as the wagons threatened to snatch, take it off and wait for the couplings to stretch. We would then bang it on and leave it so until we finally stopped, the wagons dragging us some distance before the little engine could bring them under control.

The roads here were not numbered as they were in other yards, but were called by such names as Liverpool, Bolton, Jockey Lane and the like. The roads were set, not by hand levers on the ground by shunters, but were controlled by levers in what looked like a signal box. This box, though, had no block instruments or signals, simply point rods connected to levers which were turned by a man who stayed in the box. Outside this box stood the foreman of the yard, who would shout up to the pointsman the names of the roads. The shunter, positioned in the space between the spur which linked the yard to the loop and the main line, would signal to the foreman by pointing to his liver to indicate Liverpool, touching his cap for Jockey Lane, lifting his foot knee-high to signal Bolton (where they wear the clogs) and so on; a different action for each road — a colourful system to say the least.

High above us and spanning our main line was the Cheshire Lines Railway, with its quaint selection of engines. This was only a small concern, being officially known as the Cheshire Lines Committee, using LNER locomotives but owning none of its own. It was covetously proud of its timekeeping, though, and to see these trains packed with people was a heartening sight, as it gave us the feeling we were not alone on this lovely Saturday afternoon.

At 10.20p.m. we were relieved, and when we had booked off at Dallam we wended our way home, amidst the revellers spilling out of the public houses who were completely oblivious to the fact that anyone could be working at this hour on a Saturday night. For us it was the end of our working week, some compensation being found in the knowledge that we would be on the day turn the following week.

We arrived at Arpley Shed at 8a.m. on Monday to start work on No. 13 shunt. This tiny shed consisted of two roads and came under the jurisdiction of Dallam, meaning that men could be rostered to book on or off at either. Indeed, some rosters entailed starting at one shed and then finishing at the other. When this happened it was quite a common sight to see a bicycle tied on the handrails of the running plate, so that it could be stabled at Arpley in readiness for when the man was finishing there later. This was strictly against regulations, but that did not deter most men.

Our locomotive was No. 12100, a 'Lanky'. We were to prepare her and turn off to Arpley North Siding, known to us as '2 end', our destination this strange nickname was that the code ring for this post was two long rings, three being given for the south end which was called '3 end'. The engine was 'wrong road about', so this necessitated going on to the little turntable. There was no dummy controlling this movement, so in order to reach the turntable we had to have the signalman's permission to pass the two dummies at the end of the shed, which were set at 'danger'. As there was no means of communication between engine crew and signalman, the age-old method of shouting was used.

After we had obtained his authority to proceed, we duly placed the engine and set it at a perfect balance. We then had to ask that personage in the signal box for permission again, this time to actually turn, as the buffers of our engine would be foul of the running line when the table was half-way round. Having completed the operation of turning, we again had to seek sanction to come off the table back on to the shed, this time to stop behind the dummy which would allow us to move towards 2 end, our destination. The shunter greeted us and turned us down road No. 3, the road where the wagons needing to be shunted were sent from 3 end. Shunting went on here for about three hours before we backed on to a trip (term used for a yard to yard train) then, as we were to have our meal before doing anything else, we dampered down the engine. After we had eaten our meal we left for the 'bog', this being a small yard to the back of Arpley Junction signal box. Certain roads were controlled by the signalman at Slutcher's Lane box, and a code of whistles resulted in the right points being turned. One particular road was called 'one hand', as the whistle for this was simply a single whistle or one closed fist raised aloft.

Set securely in the middle of the bog was an antiquated crane, under which we placed a wagon carrying a container which was to be unloaded. It was simply a huge baulk of timber rising obliquely from a yardwide circle of metal at ground level, held by two thick iron stays connected to a vertical stump. To the side was a large toothed wheel and a handle attached to a small wheel interlocking into the teeth of the big wheel. It was so geared that as the little wheel made a number of revolutions it impaired its power to the large wheel, which moved only a fraction of its circumference. In this way a man was able to lift weights of a ton or more. Very ingenious, but so old-fashioned.

Of the six roads on the bog, one led across the highway into the slate yard. The highway was not a busy one, but a flagman had to stand on one side to protect traffic. The road belonged to the LM&SR, and once a year the law demanded it should be roped off in order to keep its authority as prescribed in the statute book.

At the end of a tedious hour we backed on to a raft to take them to the sidings. To do this we had to drag them towards Slutcher's Lane then propel them down one-hand, then forward to the sidings. Arriving there we hooked off the engine in order to run round them to shunt. We weren't there long as it was merely a matter of tidying up, so to speak, and with a nonchalant wave of his hand and a cheery 'See you in the morning' we were despatched to the shed, our day's work completed.

The next day, around midday, George left me to go to the shunters' cabin, but before he went he told me not to put any coal on while we were standing. We hadn't a great deal to do that day so George was away for some considerable time, and knowing my mate I knew that once he started to talk he lost all sense of time. Be that as it may, I had taken him literally when he said not to put any coal on whilst standing and in consequence, when he returned to the footplate to start shunting operations, I'm afraid the humour and jokes which surround letting the fire out had become a reality; it was as dead as the proverbial dodo.

George, amiable character that he was, shouted to the shunter 'Hey lads, hey' to light her up again so we scurried round, the driver, the shunter and myself, picking up any bits of combustible material that happened to be lying about — bits of old rag, sawn-off bits of sleepers and other rubbish. These we liberally splashed with paraffin from the shunters' cabin, together with 'G' oil from our oil bottle, so it was not long before massive clouds of smoke were cascading over the sidings. This all happened before the Clean Air Act was passed, but even so, the police station was a mere stone's throw from here. We had to risk that, but soon we were able to use the blower to disperse the black smoke, allowing us to start work in a shipshape manner. When we were back to normal, George laughed as he explained what he meant when he said 'Don't put any on!', which I understood.

Saturday came and we were dispatched to the shed early, having only 'four hours in', but as was customary at Arpley Shed the chargeman said we could go (meaning book off) if we coaled her up. The coaling stage was a primitive affair in the true sense, this being a coal wagon placed on a road raised about 1ft. higher than the adjacent one. We then set our engine alongside the coal wagon, to start the arduous job of coaling it with a huge square-bladed shovel; it was hard work, but we were compensated by being able to go home long before our eight hours were completed.

Another week had passed; it was amazing how a week of 'days' passed so quickly, although the afternoon shift dragged by on leaden wings. We were working the afternoon turn the following week on No. 15 shunt, booking on at 11.40a.m. this duty being the relief to the 5.30a.m. shift we had worked on my first week as a shunting fireman. We climbed aboard the little 'Standard' at 12.35p.m. to begin this easy job which, with 55 minutes knocked off each end of the eight hours, comprised six hours ten minutes and, at 6.45p.m., we were climbing down the handrails 'straight up'.

Working up and down the shunting neck was really quite pleasant, as we had a broad view of Arpley Meadows and, beyond, the main road leading to Chester, with the quaint bridge spanning the River Mersey. Running alongside the necks was a lane known as the Half-Miler, and on such a lovely day as it was now, it was common to see American soldiers and their girlfriends making their way along this narrow lane, on their way to amorous adventures in the meadows beyond. On the nearby river, tugs and other small craft could be seen plying their way through the murky water. Just beyond the iron trellis bridge, which carried traffic bound for Chester and North Wales, the river spurred off to empty its overflow into the Manchester Ship Canal. The path of the river from the spur wound its way around the large paper mills of the Thames Board, and it was this cardboard works that now held my attention. It was a gratifying thought to imagine what it would be like inside there on a hot day, and I thanked my lucky stars that I was here on this shunting engine, with the sky as my ceiling and no walls to restrict my outdoor spirit.

So another week passed peacefully and happily although the following week we were back on 'dark days', as the night shift was often called. Our job was to sign on at the warehouse at 10.55p.m., and to take the engine to the shed just after midnight to have her coaled, watered and have the fire cleaned. This was not a pleasant job as the engine became filthy with coal and dust all over the footplate, and then again when the fire was being dropped and the ashpan was raked off. The whole operation took about two hours or longer, depending on the state of the shed at the time. Sometimes, when two big engines were being coaled, we would have a long wait, and were glad indeed when we were gonging off at the shed signal. Back at the warehouse we settled down to clean honest shunting, the rigours of the shed firmly behind us, at least for another night. Due to the time it took us on the shed, the night passed quickly, and in no time at all it seemed our relief was climbing up the hand rails; it was 5.35a.m., with another night's work completed. We had five nights on this engine, then on Saturday we were on the North End relieving at 10.20p.m.

Saturday night work was all part of our job, although most young men would scorn the idea of starting at this time. Although it neither displeased nor discouraged me, I could not help imagining what people thought as I walked along the main highway, dressed in overalls and 'chinny' (a peaked cap, with a shiny top which could be polished). Many years before it had a strap secured by two brass buttons, which could be placed under the chin when the weather was boisterous, hence the nickname. No doubt they thought I was being avaricious and doing an extra turn, but little did they realise that it was all part of our working week. Indeed, we received no extra payment except when our turn ran into Sunday, when we would be paid the enhanced rate after midnight. Often the late shift on Saturdays was an easy duty, and we spent some time in the shunters' cabin. We usually found the opportunity to indulge in a game of cards, strictly against the rules of course.

On this particular Saturday we worked hard until around 2.30a.m. when

Harry, the big, bluff and red-faced foreman told us it was time to have our supper, so we all made for the cabin where we had our meal. It was enjoyable listening to the old-timers reminiscing about their exploits in the 'good old days', when they carried buckets of fire for tail lamps, whistled 'off the shed' with their fingers and other such good-natured nonsense. All too soon, it seemed, the time came for us to go to the shed, with another week completed, and it was when we were booking off that I learned that the following week I would not be with George. This was because we had reached the bottom of the link and would now go to the top, all very well, except for one thing. The fireman went to the top of the link he had just completed, but the driver had to go into another link which contained a couple of weeks' 'spare' work. This was to keep him in touch with the main line, and maintain his route knowledge. The firemen, however, being inexperienced, stayed to work the same jobs, thus keeping in the same link. I was sorry to hear this, but George said I would be OK.

So the following Monday saw me booking on again at 5.30a.m., for the extension shunt, but with a different driver. 'Are you with me?' he asked gruffly. I nodded agreement, but I was not impressed by his lack of friendliness. Gonging off the shed, I climbed on the footplate and away we went in strained silence. I had the unmistakable feeling he did not like me.

When George had told me genially to 'put a bit on', as he called it, this driver hinted, rather sarcastically, that the 'bloody steam pressure was dropping'. This disharmony continued throughout the day, even all week, and I was glad when the week was over. It was then I realised that it would all start again on Monday. The week that followed, on No. 14 shunt, was just like the previous one; dull, boring and with no conversation, in fact it was so bad that I began to dislike my job. Even after being relieved, and when walking back to Dallam, no conversation passed between us. We booked off and went our separate ways, to begin our work the next day which to me had now become a drudge. In fact, I seriously considered changing my employment but, alas, the Government had already passed an Act called the Essential Work Order, which embraced all footplate staff. In any case, the forces would soon snap me up although, in fact, I would not have gone into the Army as my registration number ended in 'O', and all such men were destined to be 'Bevin Boys' who would spend the duration of the war in the mines. No way did I fancy going to work down a pit. Fate, therefore, decreed that I should continue on the footplate although, to be honest, life had become quite depressing.

Once, when we were shunting on the Dallam branch, my mate seemed more aggressive than ever. He stopped the engine and just stood there saying nothing, staring in front of him, and as had to happen sooner or later the shunter came and asked him what the trouble was. Came the sarcastic reply 'We'll go when we get some bloody steam'. I was amazed. I looked at the steam gauge, which indicated a pressure of 10lb. less than blowing-off point, and it then dawned on me that he was not going to move until I had put some coal into the firebox. Therefore I began to ladle it in. The needle came round and, inevitably, she began to emit steam from the safety-valves, but that is where I kept her for the next hour or so. In order to try to combat this state of affairs, he thrust the regulator open with a viciousness which made the engine slip and throw fire into the atmosphere. It was obvious that something would give, and when a spark went in my eye I'm afraid I saw red. I blew my top, calling him names which I had been brought up to scorn, and from that point onwards I knew we would never become friends.

Working together continued, and whilst on the warehouse later, we had the misfortune to have an engine with the left-hand side injector useless. Our engine was No. 7268, one of the early type that were built with no doors, no tank gauge and no hosepipe. I tried in vain to get that injector to work but then gave it up as a bad job, which meant I would have to work the other one. This involved fiddling about with the handle until it sang, but as the driver was standing with his backside close to the feed handle, and would not budge an inch, it was extremely difficult. To add to the predicament, if the brake was applied a bit hastily the injector would fly off, meaning that the shunter was in jeopardy due to the possibilty of being scalded. When this happened, I was across the footplate in a trice to shut the steam-valve off quickly. We crossed the road to fill the tank, and when it was full I let the water level fill up on the other side and then topped-up until both sides were overflowing. It was then that my cantankerous mate told me to put some more in as the boiler was not full; this when I had thrown out the heavy leather bag.

Like all things good or bad, which come to an end sooner or later, after what was seven weeks purgatory, I came to the bottom of the link. Once again I was on the extension shunt, but this time with another fresh mate. The first words he said to me were 'If your previous mate taught you nothing, I'll try'. His name was Percy, a stockily-built man in his early forties, who gave the impression that he was a person who stood no nonsense. I took a liking to this driver right away, but liked him more as I further grew to know him.

As the weeks passed I learned from him much about the rule book, on which he was quite well-read. He was also greatly interested in the steam locomotive, and taught me a whole lot about its characteristics. We had many an interesting conversation on all topics, but my great thrill came one afternoon as we were shunting the warehouse; he said he felt hungry and asked me to do the driving for a while, a chance which I jumped at. He moved over to my side of the footplate, in order to eat his sandwiches, while I stood on the driver's side with the regulator and brake under my command. I felt wonderful, and right then and there I would not have changed places with the King of England.

At first I was a little bit nervous, but after a few shunts, which I performed quite well in my own opinion, skill came with practice, and with it confidence. In no time at all I was knocking those wagons off and finding the stretch of the couplings before slamming the brake on hard, generally acting like a veteran. Percy seemed to be oblivious to my movements but I knew he was watching me and indeed, after a while, he said 'I've watched you for some time and I'll tell you something, you are not a bad judge!' This was welcome praise, as it boosted my ego and also gave back some of the confidence I thought I had lost in the seven weeks with that other so-and-so of a man.

The weeks passed by quite happily, and it was with a sense of loss that we again came to the last job in the link, once more to part and begin new acquaintances with fresh mates. My next driver was a stumpy little chap by the name of Joe Rencoe, a man who loved his beer.

Right from the start we were on the best of terms. He had a daughter the same age as myself, and perhaps this influenced his fatherly interest in me. I remember one morning when we were going to Dallam to book off, after being relieved at 11a.m., that he suggested we call at a club for a drink of beer. It was not quite opening time, but Joe gave a prearranged knock on the door and we darted inside, to be served with a couple of bottles. After the bottles it was officially time to open, so our next order was two pints. I was still not old enough by law but I thoroughly enjoyed those few pints and, I might add, they were the first of many we enjoyed in each other's company. Indeed, if the time was appropriate when we were going to relieve, or after being relieved, we always called for a couple of 'quickies'. Years later we still shared a pint or two whenever we met, which was not infrequently.

Whilst firing for Joe I did a good deal of driving, when he would curl up on my seat with a book or when he wanted his lunch. I enjoyed this and in no way could I define it as work — it was a pleasure, but at the same time it did not jeopardise my tuition in firing a locomotive. Joe taught me well, not only how to operate the engine to obtain the best results but also the theoretical points of how the steam did its work and how the valves distributed it to the cylinders, then allowing it to return through the same porthole to escape to the atmosphere. He taught me the various positions of the wheel, as it was called, this being the position of the piston head in the cylinder and the corresponding angle of the big end. He also explained the working of the injector; how it used the boiler pressure to overcome the very pressure it was using to pass water into the boiler. Thus it was with deep regret that we found ourselves at the end of our association together, when we reached the bottom job, again to part and take up duties with yet another different mate.

The early shift on the extension again saw me with a different driver, this time another stocky personality by the name of Mack Stelfox. He was a staunch teetotaller, and although he smoked, I never heard him say one word of profanity. He loved to tell stories of his exploits on the footplate but exaggerated everything to larger proportions, bordering even on the incredible. This did not detract any of the spice from the story, and in no sense could he be called a bore. My weeks firing for him were happy ones, and I was sorry to part when the time came.

This then was the pattern, first one driver then another, until just four days before my eighteenth birthday, when I was transferred to the 'rack'.

CHAPTER THREE

The Rack

The men who went into the 'rack' were drivers and firemen who were marked in the 'special link', and were referred to as 'extra men'. These men had no specific time to book on, and were called for duty at the discretion of the RSF.

The rack derived its name from a wooden contraption in which a number of blocks, some 4in. long, each bearing the name of a driver or fireman, were placed one on top of the other but displaying the name. It was placed inside the foreman's hut and was hinged for access, fitting snugly behind a small glass window, so anyone standing in the shed could see it without going into the hut. As a man finished duty he would inform the foreman as to what time he was signing off, and the foreman would then enter his name in a book, following the man who had finished immediately before him, then put his block (the one carrying his name) into the rack on top of the same man he followed in the book. In other words, the rack mirrored the book.

The man finishing did not know his next turn of duty, as he would be called when needed, any time after he had had twelve hour's rest, but by glancing at the rack a man could tell just how many men were to be called before he himself became available. The system was devised entirely for the benefit of the Management, and no outsider could possibly envisage the enormous and far-reaching consequences it involved, or the hardship it entailed. For example, suppose a man finished at, say, midday, this would mean that he would be liable for duty from midnight until 10a.m. next morning, as a maximum of ten hours was his availablility period. He would go to bed some time in the afternoon and rise again in the evening. As the time approached midnight he would be ready for work, but if he sat in the living room waiting for the 'knocker-up' he might be there all night, perhaps not being required until breakfast time. If on the other hand, he went to bed, the door knocker would be rapped maybe minutes after he snuggled into bed.

Let us suppose he finished at 6a.m. and was eligible for duty at 6p.m. in the evening until 4a.m. in the morning. This would involve him sitting at home waiting, although he may not have been required until midnight or thereabouts, with all the time he spent waiting being wasted. He could have gone to the cinema or some other place of entertainment but, alas, had he done so, he may have been needed in the late evening.

To have a bath was sometimes hazardous as, if no other member of the family was at home, he may have found himself in the embarrassing position of answering the door in a wet birthday suit. Humorous maybe, but not very funny for the man concerned. I have been in similar circumstances when it was chancy even to go to the lavatory. Ours was downstairs inside the house, but I often wondered how it would be if it was 'down the yard', as some men put it.

This, then is a brief description of the tribulations of the extra man. I worked under these conditions for 5½ years until 1946, when it was mercifully abolished.

On 5th May 1941 I was placed in the rack for the first time, receiving an availablility time of 12.05a.m., the first man out. Sure enough I was knocked to book on at 12.05a.m. Monday morning — or was it Sunday night? So I reported to the foreman on arrival at the shed, who told me to go into the cabin and wait for orders. Some forty minutes elapsed before Mr Heasom came to tell us to prepare No. 2962 for the 5a.m. Saltney service, due off the shed at 4.30a.m.

This was a distasteful job at any time, but Sunday night into Monday morning was actually the worst time. The shed was full of locomotives which had been freshy fired, with black and yellowish smoke oozing out of the chimneys and lazily hanging about in the air, filling the shed with thick, dense smoke which hurt the lungs with each intake of breath. Visibility was down to a few feet, and as the sole source of illumination came from dimly-lit gas lights, one can easily imagine how difficult it was to even discern the floor.

Each alternate road was stunted with pillars, each about 8ft. apart, which held up the roof. Down the other five roads were hydrant holes bearing a lid 2ft. across, but when these were in use the lid could not be replaced in position, so to walk down one of these roads was as precarious as a sapper going through a minefield.

To assist us in our unenviable task, I went to the stores and obtained a duck lamp. This was a small paraffin-filled tin vessel with a long spout, out of which protruded worsted wool saturated by the paraffin which, when lit, gave off huge clouds of black smoke which smelt awful. No doubt the 'Wise and Foolish Virgins' used similar ones all those years ago. Carrying a bucket of tools and a shovel, while holding this lamp aloft, I made my way to the engine we were to prepare; the lamp had to be held aloft, otherwise it would blur our view of the floor. I found No. 2962 and threw the bucket and shovel on to the footplate, then clambered aboard.

She had just been coaled and the footplate was littered with coal, the lumps being the size of boulders. Although the firehole door was shut, flames were belching through the cracks and the cab was full of smoke. Stepping gingerly over the debris, I shot a well-aimed kick at the blower, which immediately sucked away the menacing flames while another well-placed kick, this time with the sole of my boot, made the firehole door shoot open. I periously climbed up the tender to extricate the dart — no mean feat, as coal had wedged it firmly in the sockets. I somehow managed to dislodge it then, drawing it back, I turned it round so that the business end was pointing towards the firebox and thrust it in the fire. Pushing and heaving against unburnt coal, I spread it round the firebox, and then it was the acrobatic performance to replace the dart from whence it came.

The next job was to shift the coal and, with the aid of the coalpick, I set about and threw it, by hand, into the firebox. It was easy now to scrape the small pieces with the shovel, and then to brush the footplate, making it much easier to move about the cab. The next thing was to find two lamps and trim them, along with a gauge lamp, all of which I purloined from stabled engines. This was quite a common practice, as the stores were invariably inadequately stocked. After going down the shed to obtain oil, I mounted the framing to fill the numerous oil boxes dotted alongside the boiler. Meanwhile, the driver was busy lubricating the motion, and when we were finished, we both made for the tap at the bottom of No. 2 road, to clean up before we adjourned to the cabin.

To sit in the cabin in the early hours was something of an ordeal. As we had been out of bed all day Sunday, we were tired, and it was not long before our heads began to rest on elbows in a sitting position, at first, with the head gradually sinking on to folded arms flat on the table. No sooner had I relaxed in a comfortable position than Mr Heasom's baritone voice was booming down our earholes to get No. 5630 ready for the 6a.m. Carlisle. Gosh! It was bad enough preparing a 'Black Five', but a Class 5XP, as No. 5630 was, had three cylinders and required oiling 'underneath'. To accomplish this the locomotive had to be set, first of all, with the big end at one o'clock, so that the crosshead was then at an angle to accept the oil. To pour in the oil was a real test of agility, as the crosshead was some 10ft. or more above the floor of the pit. Placing the duck lamp on the slide-bar above my head, and then the tallowpot, I scrambled on to the side of the pit, holding on to any part of the motion that I could, and then hauling myself up by hand power, managed to place my feet on the slippery connecting rods. Three hands were needed, one to hold the duck lamp, another to pour the oil, and yet another to hold the precarious position high above the pit bottom. Many times in the future, I would know that exasperating feeling when the tallowpot would slip from its greasy perch, or the duck lamp would be knocked flying, to render total darkness in which to negotiate the zigzag descent, in order to retrieve the wretched lamp and perhaps go down to the shed and refill it again.

I finished the crosshead and then descended, only to ascend once more to a lofty height, close to the big end, eccentrics, and other oiling points which were housed so secretly under the belly of the boiler. Afterwards, it was back to No. 2 road to clean up again. In the hope that we wouldn't have to prepare another engine, we hurried to the warmth and comparative comfort of the cabin to have a welcome cup of tea and a sandwich. Although bread and cheese at 4a.m. in the morning was not very palatable we were, nevertheless, hungry, and somehow managed to appease our dubious appetites. Shortly after 5a.m. the foreman told us to relieve the Mold Junction to Bamfurlong service; a train that was worked by our own men who had worked out to Mold Junction but were now on overtime, due to delay.

Climbing on the Stanier 'Black Five' we had the usual chat about the load and who the guard was, and we then set off down the slow line towards Winwick Junction. Here we waited for a couple of expresses to pass before being allowed out on to the main line, for the railroad to the north was only 'up' and 'down' to Golborne Junction, where it opened into four roads again. Here we were turned on to the slow line and, after stopping at Golborne Station for signals, then again at Cross Tetleys, we continued to Bamfurlong Sidings, where we dropped down a steep gradient, at the bottom of which were trap points. Stopping at the bottom I hooked the engine off the train, put a lamp on the tender and waited for the signal. When it was lowered we drew forward to go behind a dummy on the West Loop in readiness to run to Dallam Shed. This meant running tender first and, coupled with the fact that we were tired and cold, we were glad indeed when we reached the shed. Berthing her we lost no time in putting the shovel and bucket of tools in the stores, and booked off at 9.30a.m. while I put myself in the rack, and received a paper for 9.30p.m.

Arriving home I had a light snack and a wash, before quickly retiring to the 'Land of Nod'. I slept throughout the day, and had just finished my evening meal when a knock at the door resulted in my booking on at 10.30p.m., as required. This was still Monday, yet here I was starting my second turn, but as we had no specific job we sat in the cabin to await instructions. It was around midnight when we were ordered to walk to Winwick Quay, to relieve our own men on the 'Abrams'. This train started away from Froghall at 6.25p.m., then shunted at Kenyon and later continued to Abram Colliery in the Wigan Coalfield. Quite a lot of shunting was done at the colliery, which was a very dark and dismal place and was known by the men as the 'Black Hole of Calcutta'.

Winwick Quay is about a mile north of Dallam, but it would take all of the 45 minutes allowed to walk down Winwick Road, the way we were supposed to walk. Arriving at the Quay we found our train was behind another on the loop; this was not unusual, as the loops were signalled under the 'permissive block' regulations and a goods train could be put behind another, so long as the driver was warned by the signalman, who would exhibit a green hand-signal to indicate the line was not clear to the next stop signal. Our engine was an 0-8-0, a 'Super D', so-called because it was superheated, having element tubes running through the smoke tubes, thus heating the steam to a greater temperature.

The coal on the tender was well back, so my first job, once we had settled on the footplate, was to climb up and throw it forward. By this time the train in front had run 'right over' to shunt, so my mate drew up to the home signal. This entailed waiting until the train had finished shunting, so my mate and I went into the shunters' cabin at the side of the signal box. An hour elapsed before we could draw our own train over the points to shunt, and eventually to back up on a raft of coal wagons for Dallam. All this took time, and it was daylight when we arrived at South End Yard to break our train up in the various roads. On completion of this we took the engine on to the shed, finishing at 7.15a.m., and with yet another shift completed I was now available for my next turn, at 7.15p.m. that evening.

That night I began duty at 8p.m., this time getting a job almost right away. My mate on this trip was a well-groomed individual, and although I had not fired for him before, I liked him immediately, and found him to be an interesting person. We enjoyed good conversation, and during the run to Preston, on this occasion, we had a good old natter when we were held at signals along the road. His name was Jack Locke, and I felt at ease with him, unlike some other drivers who made a fireman feel inferior. We were relieved upon our arrival at Preston, and when we had finished our food we were to relieve a Carlisle to Warrington train, a through freight from Carlisle terminating at Winwick Quay.

The freight train arrived at Preston at 1.40a.m. headed by 'Black Five' No. 5321, an engine shedded at Dallam. These engines were the favourites of all the locomotive men on the LMS system, and although it was my first time on this class, I soon found out how good they were. The footplate was comfortable and roomy, with a seat, and although the latter doubled as the oilbox lid, it was big enough to fit the entire backside, and was positioned under the side window to allow a clear look-out in the sitting position. The right-hand injector worked off exhaust steam, my first experience of this type, but my mate showed me how to open the steam-valve gradually, then to whip it round fast to pick up the water, making the injector purr like a kitten. Firing her was comparatively easy, too, as the firebox sloped towards the front end, and the art of good steaming was to keep her warm at the back corners and thinning gently down the box to the front.

She ran freely, and with the 6ft. driving wheels she made excellent progress up the steep incline to Bank Top Cottages. From here we dropped down to Standish, where we were turned over the Whelley Line. This was a common manoeuvre as the line avoided the station at Wigan, and most goods trains ran over this switchback road which joined the main line again at Bamfurlong. Working a train over this undulating track, however, was extremely difficult, and Jack told me of the perils of breaking apart and the way to overcome them. It was very interesting; first we dropped down an incline and then up another, only to be at the top of another hill all the way to Bamfurlong.

Here we were let out on to the slow line, after which we proceeded to Golborne Junction to wait for more important trains to pass. When they had gone by we were let out to run down the two road stretch to Winwick Junction, to be turned into the loop to the Quay. We were then brought to a stand before the signal was lowered with the 'bobby' (signalman) giving us a green hand signal, sticking his forefinger in the air indicating that there was 'one in front'. Therefore Jack proceeded cautiously, as he had to bring our train to a gentle stop behind the one standing at Winwick Quay 'up' slow home. There was also an engine shunting the yard, and until he had finished his work there was nothing we could do. Even when he backed up for 'right away' we still had to wait for the one in front of us to do likewise.

Whilst sitting on a locomotive under the night sky, with the glare from the firehole illuminating a tiny area around the footplate and only the sound of whispering steam in the silent countryside, two men are invariably drawn into conversation. The topics were wide and varied, depending on the character of the individuals. I learned to love times like these, and have enjoyed immensely similar situations in the years that followed. Thus we passed the time pleasantly, and upon looking forward, presently, my mate suddenly declared with a grin that we were 'first up'.

The shunter here was recognised as being a 'good lad with a stick', and in no time at all he had those wagons running hither and thither. Our last duty was to run light engine to the depot, finishing at 5.50a.m., and on Wednesday evening I booked on for the bank engine at 7.25p.m. This duty was in a 'regular' link, and comprised firemen who were all passed for driving. The object of manning these local jobs with passed firemen was to give quick access in case a driver was needed in a hurry, as the RSF could easily send a passed cleaner to relieve him as he was always within walking distance of the shed. Tonight, however, the regular fireman of the banker was 'brought off' as he booked on, hence I. was knocked for the job to replace him. He was required for a main line train, and was given a more experienced fireman than myself.

The driver who I was to fire for was a man of slight stature called Ephraime Smith, who left no one in any doubt that he was henpecked. Despite this he had a wonderful sense of humour, not particular witty but oh, so dry! We walked down the road to Arpley, to wait in No. 28 cabin for our engine to come down the bank. The cabin had been called No. 28 for so many years that the origin of the nickname had faded into obscurity.

The 'bank engine', usually parked on Arpley Shed, had easy access to a train needing assistance from the junction up the 1 in 69 gradient to Acton Grange. The big bridge spanning the Manchester Ship Canal was the summit of the climb, and it was here that the banker left the train and then drifted behind him to reach the box. Here, he would cross over to the opposite running line, to make his way back to Arpley ready for the next one to assist.

Our locomotive was No. 7729, a 5ft. 6in. side tank coal engine. There was very little room to move about on the footplate, and I was glad I didn't have a driver with a broad buffer beam. She carried a limited amount of water, and the tank would require filling twice on this shift. The brake was worked by vacuum, operated by a push-in lever at the back of the regulator handle. The firebox was small, and had to be stacked thickly under the door and back corners, with the exhaust and smoke going up a chimney some 3ft. high.

Reaching Acton Grange, after pushing a heavy tank train, my mate let it gradually pull away from us, then drifted at a safe distance behind the signal box. The dummy came off and we came back down the bank, past Walton Old Junction to Arpley, where we parked out of the way on the small shed. It was much later when we went behind the next train, and Ephraime gave two 'crows' on the whistle to indicate that we were in position to start pushing. Back came the answering 'crows', so we set about pushing as hard as our little engine could. It was dark by now, and when we reached the top of the bank and dropped down to the box, I changed the buffer lamps, taking out the red shade from the rear and putting it in the one which would now become the tail light. We banked another train afterwards and then, at about 2.30a.m., we screwed on the handbrake and left her, to walk the lonely road back to Dallam.

At noon I was up and about again, having had a good six hours sleep, and as I was not available for work until 3.25p.m. I took a stroll in the nearby park. It was a lovely day and I sat by the bowling green watching a number of contests, chiefly between elderly men. Two of the men playing bowls were drivers, and I acknowledged the wave of their hands. At length, one of these packed his bowls in his bag and made off; I had to be going too, as I had to be home when the knocker-up came.

On arriving home my mother prepared a meal for me, and no sooner had I finished it, when the knocker sounded; I was to book on at 4p.m., as required. When booking myself on duty I was met by Tommy Roughsedge, one of the bowlers that I had been watching earlier, and he informed me that he was my mate. We were told to sit in the cabin and await instructions, and within half an hour the RSF told us to walk to Bank Quay Station to relieve a train for Mold Junction.

The engine was a Class 5XP, a three cylinder locomotive with 6ft. 9in. driving wheels. This was the first time on this class for me, but I was immediately impressed by this beautiful piece of machinery. The beat, when we climbed the bank to Acton Grange, was rather muffled, the reason for this being the three cylinders, but topping the ship canal, however, when she gained speed, the beat became more distinctive, and three clear puffs came from the exhaust on each half turn of the wheel. When going at about 30m.p.h. the rhythm changed to a clear one-two-three, one-two-three, with each revolution of the massive wheel. The firebox seemed endless when I looked into the fire, and I wondered how on earth I would put coal to the front end of this terribly long grate. Somehow I managed to do this and, after a few fires round the box, I began to enjoy riding on this footplate, even leaning over the cabside, feeling the wonderfully smooth running of this greyhound of a locomotive.

We were now approaching Norton Tunnel, with smoke pouring from the black mouth and up over the lovely Cheshire landscape, and with a snort and a sinister roar she plunged her chimney into that gaping blackness. Keeping steam on for a few hundred yards then closing the regulator, not forgetting to put the blower to work just beforehand, she ran all the way through the tunnel to plunge into daylight just before the small country station of Halton. Our signal was still at 'danger', so Tommy brought the train to a stand a few yards short of the gantry which carried a small arm for the loop, as well as for the home signal.

A diamond on the signal post would mean the line was track-circuited, with a tell-tale indicator in the box, but as there was no such diamond here I was obliged to go to the box, as per rule, remind the signalman where we were standing and then sign the train register book, as proof of carrying out the rule. The loop was clear, and we could see no apparent reason why we could not be turned into it, but after couple of minutes had elapsed I set off to the box. No sooner had I returned to the footplate than the small arm was lowered for us to go inside; had this been done a little earlier it would have saved me a fruitless journey, although this sort of behaviour was by no means unusual.

When given a little steam by my mate, the big-wheeled locomotive ground round the bend away from the main line, and drifted down the loop to the far end, coming to a halt a few feet from the trap points which guarded the intrusion on to the main line. Beyond the traps was a sheer drop of some 40ft. where, far below, a highway ran parallel with the River Weaver, which itself ran alongside a canal. The line traversed this valley over a twelve arch viaduct, then dipped slightly towards Frodsham.

We were being held here for a passenger train to pass from the Runcorn direction, the signals for this train being in the 'off' position. This line joined ours almost at a right angle, and had a speed restriction of 15m.p.h. After the passenger train had passed and cleared the starting signal we were let out of the loop, and were soon on our way to Frodsham. After passing through this well-kept station, the line levelled out over the flat Cheshire countryside to Helsby, and the sininster-looking hill, overlooking this rural station from the east, took on the silhouette of a man's face as we approached. From here the line inclined, so I spread a round of coal on the thin fire, sufficient to take us up this light bank. Again she took on the rhythmic sound of her six beats, as she gallantly climbed towards Dunham Hill, and once again we were transferred to the loop to await another passenger train — this time from Manchester. Apart from the hotel, located high over to the east, there was nothing here, and in the gathering dusk and the silence of the country it was, indeed, lonely.

It was now about 9.30p.m., and after the Manchester passenger train had gone we set off on the last lap, so to speak, to Chester. From here the line was almost level for a mile or so but then it rose steeply, past Mickle Trafford, to Guildon Sutton, a nondescript box perched right on the top of the incline, where the line dropped steeply down a 1 in 100 gradient to a sharp bend at the bottom. Immediately beyond this 15m.p.h. curve was a maze of semaphore signals, heralding the entrance to Chester. Here a driver had to know his road, as a signal taken wrongly could have disastrous consequences. I also mused how on earth I would ever learn to read these, as each one led to a different road.

On the two signal gantry we first encountered, the right-hand signal was 'clear', and Tommy told me to look out for the next which was on the 'blind side'. I shouted to him that the third from the left was 'off', then looked for one entirely on its own, as my driver instructed. This one was 'clear' too; we were going on through the goods line. I saw two signals on the next gantry, with the left-hand one 'off', and then I was to look for one near No. 4 box, left hand again, another one a bit further on and then finally the home signal for No. 6 box. The railroad twisted and turned all the way through Chester and, after passing No. 6 box, we plunged into a short four road tunnel, shooting out of this only to be engulfed almost at once by another, this one covering two roads. Emerging from this, we passed Crane Street box, then rumbled over the iron bridge spanning the River Dee. We then ran on to Saltney Junction, where we were switched over to the slow line. This somehow puzzled me, but Tommy explained that from Chester No. 6 box to Saltney Junction the fast lines ran parallel, with the slow lines running parallel on the right. At the junction, however, the slow lines were on the left all the way to Mold Junction where they changed again.

Upon reaching Mold Junction we kept to the left, with the main line veering off to the right. Running right past the shunters' cabin we stopped, and then I looked back for the guard's hand signal which would authorise us to set back into the sidings. Gently my mate propelled the train into the sidings, clear of the adjacent roads, and here I hooked the engine off and proceeded to the shed. We left the engine on the turntable, to be turned later by the shed men. Upon reporting to the RSF, we were told to go home with the Mold Junction to Rowsley working which would be leaving in about half an hour. This meant we would be riding in the brake van to Arpley, so we made our way across to the yard we had just come from and found the train. Climbing into the brake, we told the guard of our intentions, then made ourselves comfortable and ready for the journey to our home station. Arriving at Arpley at 12.55a.m., we walked to Dallam and booked off at 1.50a.m.

Friday afternoon saw me booking on at 2p.m., as required; we were ordered to walk to Arpley, to relieve a train for Edge Hill. Climbing aboard

'Crab' No. 2772, at 3.45p.m., we set off towards Crossfield Crossing. Going under the main line at Warrington (Low Level) the line veered to the right, and obscured the signals until we were only about 30 yards from them. When we did see them in the 'clear' position, Stan, my mate, started to gather the train on a tight coupling by opening the regulator, slightly at first, but when all the couplings were tight he piled on more steam in order to negotitate the short sharp climb to Monks Hall box. From Monks Hall the road was flat to Carterhouse where it rose steeply over a knoll, before reaching Widnes No. 7, then dropped away gently to the small junction at West Deviation. A little further on our line ducked under the main London to Liverpool line, to converge at Ditton. Keeping to the slow line, we climbed the stiff gradient to a high level. There were troughs here, but Stan informed me that it was futile to try to obtain water from them because, being on top of the bank, they were badly situated and were no good anyway.

From Hale Bank the road started to climb in earnest, and was 'up bank' all the way to Edge Hill. I had to fire this 'Crab' continually, and she rocked from side to side with each pull of her pistons, but she clanked noisily onward, scornful of the heavy load. Passing Edge Hill No. 11, the box controlling access to and from the shed, we began the steady crawl round the half-circle stretch of line that terminated on the sidings at Tuebrook. Hooking off the engine, and putting the lamps right for our return trip back along this half-circle to No. 11 box, we went forward over the points and were called back by the shunter. Upon reaching the shed box we had to do a set back movement, before we were put towards the shed bank. This was steep, indeed, and it was with the utmost caution that Stan gently eased our engine down this gradient. The bank itself was barely three engine-lengths long, and we had to stop clear at the bottom. Eventually we were called off by the man in charge, and when we reached his cabin he simply said 'Nudge her, Warrington!' The 'Warrington' was a friendly salutation to men from other depots, calling the men by their home station. The 'nudge her', however, was something entirely different because it meant we were to dispose of the locomotive, drop the fire, clean the smokebox and ashpan, coal her, the lot! Purely a distasteful job.

Placing the engine on the ash pit, I stopped my mate when the tank filling-hole was level with the water-column and then set about filling the tank — a masterpiece of agility. Clambering up the single rail on the side of the tender, I swung round to the back, to gain access to the top by climbing on the step. Surrounding the tank lid was an area about 3ft. square, and although two drain-holes were fixed in the bottom of this to allow water to escape, these were almost always blocked with small pieces of coal; consequently there was the inevitable spillage, some 6in. deep. As the fireman had to stand here in order to pull up the heavy hose bag, a couple of lumps of coal were usually placed in strategic positions to accommodate the feet. Swinging over the lip of the tender, I dexterously sought these large chunks with my feet. Unless they had been carefully selected they would be uneven, and would deposit me ankle-deep in the water when they wobbled. Standing precariously on these makeshift footholds, I had to reach out and grab the chain in synchronisation with Stan when he swung it towards me. Taking hold of the chain with one hand, and holding the tender with the other, I adjusted my stance to establish more security. I then pulled up the hose bag, which felt like it weighed a ton, wrestled it up over the rim of the tender and then manhandled the business end into the tank. Shouting to my mate 'to turn it on', I kept a wary eye open for punctures in the leather, as this caused jets of water to spout indiscriminately upwards and sidewards, so I had to be ready to dodge this to ensure dry trousers. The tank filled in a few minutes, and when turned off, the same agile operation had to be reversed. Now, however, the bag was full of water, due to the sag of the bag from the rim of the tender to the raised lid. The best way was to lift the water-laden bag up and let the water drain into the tank, but doing this from the unstable perch of two coal blocks was no mean feat. Even when this had been achieved, there was still the difficulty of heaving that big, cumbersome, heavy, wet and slippery bag over the side, to land in a cascade of water round the bottom of the column.

Placing the engine over the pit I then found the 'dukes', a large pair of tongs with which to pull out the firebars. I placed these alongside the footplate and climbed aboard. Meanwhile, Stan had been busy with the paddle, and had pushed most of the fire to one side. Then, by dislodging the clinker with the dart, I put the tongs in the firebox. It was no easy job grasping the bars with these, but I managed and, when I was sure I had a good enough grip on one, I brought the tongs down heavily on the firehole ring thus uprooting the stubborn bar. Another heave and it was clear of its counterparts. Then, holding the tongs in a firm grip, I at last manoeuvred them and the bar through the firehole and on to the footplate. Exasperating work! That was the first, but three more had to follow before we could start to rake the fire through the hole and into the ashpan. The tool we used for this was an iron rake, an implement that seemed a lot longer than it really was. Pulling the fire through, and then pushing it as far as we could along the ashpan, with sweat dripping off the end of our noses, we took a turn each, one recovering his breath while the other pushed and heaved. At last most of the dirty fire had been pushed into the ashpan so now I had to go down into the pit, still armed with the long rake, and begin the loathsome task of raking the ash out of the pan into the pit.

If the wind was blowing from the right direction it wasn't so bad, but if it was in front, then each pull of the rake resulted in being covered with hot ash. On this occasion it was not too bad, although hot ash and fumes were not very palatable at any time. Sticking gamely to my task I cleared the ashpan and climbed on the footplate, to replace those bars we dislodged earlier. This job was just as cumbersome as the operation of lifting them out, and great care had to be taken in case the bars fell into the ashpan; if this happened, it was the devil's own work to retrieve them. Replacing them at last, we scattered some coal on the remaining fire, to keep the grate warm, and then drew forward to clean the somkebox. Taking the big spanner and the shovel I climbed on the 'piano', the flat ledge above the bogies. Here I slackened the numerous nuts that secured the smokebox door then swung it open, only to get covered in smokebox ashes. This was soon done and, after closing the door and securing it tight, I threw the shovel to the ground and descended.

Our next job was to berth her, and on completion of this we filled the shovel with water from the boiler and proceeded to wash our hands. The

1 A view of Warrington (Dallam) locomotive shed, photographed in the mid-1960s.

S. Cheetham

2 Ex-LMS Ivatt 2-6-0 Class 4, No. 43047, simmers at Arpley Junction Shed on 3rd January 1966. By this time No. 43047 (a Heaton Mersey-allocated locomotive) had lost its smokebox numberplate.

S. Cheetham

3 'Black Five' No. 45256 stands outside the shed building at Warrington (Dallam) Shed.

S. Cheetham

4 Ex-LMS Stanier Mogul, No. 42983, is pictured at Winwick Quay on 15th August 1963, whilst hauling a freight train.

S. Cheetham

5 Slutcher's Lane signal cabin and, in the background, Warrington (Bank Quay) Station.
N. Coates

6 Froghall Bridge, north of Warrington; the main line from Warrington to Wigan passes beneath.
S. Cheetham

7 The brick-built Dunham Massey signal cabin, in April 1974, situated on the ex-LNWR line between Warrington and Timperley on the ex-MSJ&A line to Manchester.

V. R. Anderson

8 An L&YR Aspinall 2F, No. 12172, is pictured at Golborne with a short freight.

V. R. Anderson Collection

9 Ex-LMS 'Jubilee' No. 5573 *Newfoundland* passes Golborne with the 6.25a.m. mixed freight from Carlisle to Crewe.

British Rail

10 No. 45562 *Alberta*, one of the last surviving ex-LMS 'Jubilees' in BR revenue-earning service, being finally allocated to Holbeck, hauls a Lancaster (Green Ayre) to Manchester freight near Carlisle Bridge.

V. R. Anderson

11 Ladies Walk signal and box as seen in April 1966.
V. R. Anderson

12 Ladies Walk Sidings, Lancaster, showing the marshalling facilities, and the city in the background, on 12th April 1966.
V. R. Anderson

13 A Holbeck-based 8F, No. 48157 approaches Ladies Walk with a train
of box vans on 12th April 1966.

V. R. Anderson

14 Interesting rolling stock, hauled by 'Royal Scot' class 4-6-0 No. 46103
Royal Scots Fusilier, makes up a stopping train at Lancaster.

J. Coltas

15 This view of Lancaster (Castle) Station shows the impressive buildings.

British Rail

16 A view of Lancaster (Castle) Station, with 'Princess Coronation' class Pacific No. 46250 *City of Lichfield*, seen departing.

British Rail

17 An ex-LMS 'Black Five', No. 45265, filling the sky with black smoke, hauls a mixture of cattle wagons and tank wagons through Lancaster (Castle) Station on 23rd August 1967.

V. R. Anderson

18 The small signal cabin, which stands on the end of Lancaster (Green Ayre) Station, with it short wooden staircase.

V. R. Anderson Collection

19 Overhead electric wires feature at Lancaster (Green Ayre) Station in April 1966.

V. R. Anderson

20 No. 43027, an ex-LMS 2-6-0 4F, allocated to Carnforth, shown by both the shed plate (10A) and the stencilled name on the buffer beam, runs 'wrong line' at Lancaster (Green Ayre) to reach New Zealand Sidings in April 1966.

V. R. Anderson

21 Holbeck-allocated 8F, No. 48157, is pictured at Lancaster (Green Ayre) in April 1966.

V. R. Anderson

22 A general view of Lancaster (Green Ayre) Shed, on 20th June 1965, showing the shed buildings, track layout and, in the background, the station.

V. R. Anderson

23 In 1946, the LMS introduced the 2F 2-6-0 locomotive and No. 46422 is pictured leaving the shed yard at Lancaster (Green Ayre) in 1966.

V. R. Anderson

24 No. 45354, a 'Black Five', protrudes into the sunlight from the darkness of Lancaster (Green Ayre) Shed on 20th June 1965.

V. R. Anderson

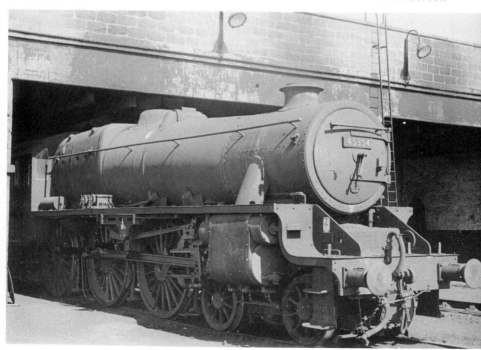

25 No. 48305 approaches Morecambe (Euston Road) with a freight. The locomotive is devoid of a shed plate.

V. R. Anderson

26 Morecambe (Euston Road) Station, in February 1967, with 'Black Five' No. 45111 preparing to take on her next duty.

V. R. Anderson

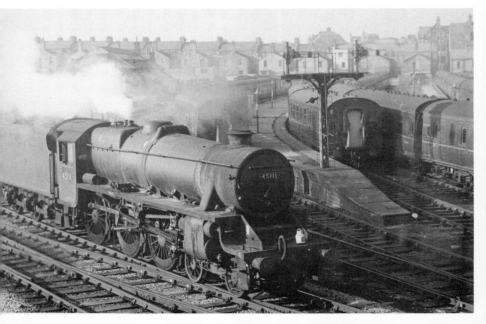

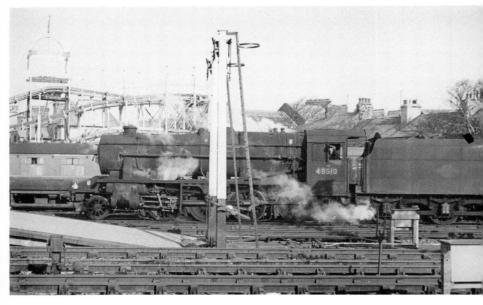

27 With the amusement park in the background, 8F No. 48510 waits at the end of Morecambe (Promenade) Station.

V. R. Anderson

28 A deserted Morecambe (Promenade) Station, with ex-LMS 'Black Five' No. 45014 approaching the yards, in February 1967. This view shows one of the non-electrified platforms.

V. R. Anderson

29 The 'up' 'Mid-Day Scot', hauled by 'Princess Royal' class 4-6-2 *Princess Elizabeth*, steams through Hest Bank on a dull day.

V. R. Anderson Collection

30 A northbound mineral train, hauled by 'Black Five' No. 45424, is pictured at Hest Bank on 21st August 1967.

V. R. Anderson

31 With camping coaches in the background, an ex-LMS 'Black Five', No. 45285, hauls 'Presflo' wagons through Hest Bank Station on 21st August 1967.

V. R. Anderson

32 'Black Five' No. 44868, devoid of smokebox number plate and with 9B shed code painted on, simmers at Carnforth Shed beside 0-6-0 diesel shunter No. D4140.

V. R. Anderson

fact that the water was scalding hot did not deter us for, with a sort of slapping movement with the flat of the hand, the water did not have time to scald us. This was the way we cleaned up before we were ready to leave. We were to travel home as passengers but we had to walk to Edge Hill to catch our train, rather a long walk from the shed. We had not long to wait and soon we were booking off at Dallam, at 12.15a.m.

Next day was Saturday and I was knocked to book on at 12.15p.m., after a mere twelve hours rest. Upon arriving at the depot I found my mate was Joe Rencoe, my old mate on a shunting engine. We were to prepare Warrington 'Black Five' No. 5252, turn off to Froghall and work a special to Amberswood. This was only ten miles from Warrington, but during the dark days of the war the railways were saturated to capacity, and hours were spent waiting for a road behind other trains.

Taking the left-hand road at Bamburlong we travelled over the Whelley line, past Platt Bridge, and on to Amberswood West. Here we veered to the right, and shunted our train into the sidings. When the train was properly disposed of we then went in a tender first direction to Amberswood East then, when we were over the appropriate points, we set off to Bamfurlong engine first; we had turned the locomotive round the triangle which formed the layout of the railroad. Now it was plain sailing for the run to Dallam Shed, where we stabled the engine and signed off duty. The time now was 8.50p.m. and, because of the double summer time which was operated during the war, it was still daylight and quite pleasant to be finishing before darkness.

As it was too late to go home to change out of working clothes, Joe and I adjourned to Annie's, the little pub across the branch. This was quite customary for Dallam men who finished work in the late evening, so we fully expected to meet some of our men inside. Sure enough, there were several drivers and a couple of firemen indulging in a drop of beverage, and soon we formed a school of dominoes, playing on the white-scrubbed table. This kind of relaxation was really enjoyable, and time sped by on fleeting wings. All conception of time evaporated, and it was a disappointment when Annie's melodious voice informed all and sundry 'last orders'. Jumping up, Joe dashed to the bar to secure two pints and then we settled down for the remaining few games. All too soon we were bidding each other hearty 'goodnights' outside, then we dispersed, each man going his own way.

This, then, was the end of my first week in the 'rack' and, as I meandered my way home, I could not help reflecting on the turns I had performed, seven in all, in the last six days. Two Monday turns, both at night, a couple of late evenings then afternoons, and apart from being rather late, today's shift could be called 'days'. I now had a paper time for 3p.m. Sunday; at least I would have a night in bed.

A couple of weeks later I joined the LMS contingent of the Local Defence Volunteers. This comprised an army of volunteers who undertook to guard the local area generally, and their own place of employment in particular. As for us, we were pledged to protect the railway premises surrounding Warrington.

CHAPTER FOUR

The Home Guard

Our headquarters were at Arpley station, and our parade ground was Arpley Cricket Ground. It was well-mown where cricket was played, but the part on which we did our 'Square-bashing' was covered with tufted grass about 6in. high. The officers were from the clerical staff and Control Office, an arrangement not based on logic but on the old school tie. The sergeants, mostly drivers and goods guards, with an odd one or two from other grades were, without exception, men who had served in World War I.

The officers were quite amiable, but it was the sergeants with their own brand of humour who made the routine of army life and training bearable. Our evenings were utilised in drilling, marching and how to handle a rifle. We had lectures on different types of arms; the Lee Enfield, the anti-tank weapon, the E.Y. rifle, the Browning Automatic and perhaps a few more. I found these classes very interesting and some quite entertaining even, depending on which NCO was the tutor. At weekends we were assigned to digging trenches around the Warrington area, all on railway property. Occasionally, we would go to Thelwall for a weekend camp, and also on our curriculum was a night guard duty which each man would do about once or twice a month.

The guard consisted of one man from each platoon, six in all. Thus a railwayman, a soapworks employee and a foundry worker would find themselves doing a guard alongside a wire-weaver, an aluminium processor and a forgeman. Bunks were provided at the places we were ordered to guard, but I'm afraid the lure of a pack of cards was a greater temptation than the more necessary functions of slumberland, and we usually succumbed all too easily. Therefore, firing an engine immediately after coming off guard was a battle against fatigue.

We learned about the .22 rifle and later the .303. Now and then, on a Sunday morning, we would be marched in ranks to Longford Rifle Range where we would fire ten rounds each, under the supervision of Army personnel. Sometimes we would go to an open field, on the marshy land adjacent to the Mersey, a place known as the Sandy Desert. There was no sand here, only silt dredged from the river bed, but it was called 'desert' because nothing grew on it — it was a barren wilderness, totally removed from civilisation, an ideal place to explode hand grenades. The first time I went there I was under the command of Sergeant Garner, a driver with whom I was not too well acquainted. We gathered round him as he explained what was expected of us.

'First', he barked 'pull the grenade off the pin, not the pin from the grenade! It is perfectly harmless until you let go of the spring-loaded catch. As soon as you do, you have four seconds before it explodes. So don't worry, as you take the grenade from the pin with your right hand look at your target, take aim, then lob it over. When you've lobbed it look where it lands, counting four seconds from the time it leaves your hand before you duck!'

We were then herded into an enclosure some 4 yards square, surrounded by sandbags stacked about 4ft. high. Sergeant Garner then took each man separately, stood with him behind the wall of sandbags and instructed him to throw the grenade at the target some 20 yards away.

'Pin out!'

'Right Serg.'

'Aim! Throw!'

'Right Serg.'

'Look where it lands. One . . . Two . . . Three . . . Down!'

I knew exactly what to do when my turn came; pin out, aim and throw. I threw all right and started counting too, but it did not take me four seconds to count to four. No sir, more like four hundredths of a second, then I ducked. The sergeant pulled me up by the scruff of the neck and told me to look where it landed, but by now, the four seconds had elapsed, and we both had to duck. The exercise ended happily, and some of the lads had a good laugh later at my expense, but it was all good clean fun. After we were dismissed we took up most of the room in the nearby Roe Buck Hotel, as was our usual custom after Sunday morning parades.

When weather permitted we often went for a Sunday route march. These were nearly always pleasant affairs, as we invariably stopped for a drink en route. We were marching back on one such occasion when Arthur, the sergeant in charge, ordered us to march with rifles at the 'slope'. This was all very well, but after shouldering a rifle for mile after mile our arms began to ache. Mine ached terribly, but I knew I was not on my own. A number of the lads were bemoaning their fate until one, perhaps slightly braver than the rest, said 'Hey, Arthur, our bloody arms are dropping off!' Arthur, a goods guard and a likeable person, said 'Oops, sorry lads, I clean forgot about you' and immediately ordered us to march at the trail. Alas, as my arm came down to transfer the rifle it was muscle-locked, and my rifle was retrieved only by a superhuman effort. However, everything ended satisfactorily.

One Saturday I remember in particular was when I booked on at 4.35 a.m. to work the 6.15a.m. stopping train to Bolton. Our locomotive was already prepared, being due off the shed at 4.50a.m. to perform some coach shunting beforehand. We stopped at ten stations, including the notorious Chequerbent Bank, and upon leaving Atherton Station we faced a climb of 1 in 24, which even a Class 4P passenger tank engine found taxing to the utmost. It was not unusual to stick here, especially on Monday mornings when the rails were covered with weekend rust. Reaching Bolton (Great Moor Street) I had to disconnect the vacuum-pipes, steam-heater pipes and the oil-stained shackle, before proceeding to Plodder Lane Shed to turn the engine. We then went back to Great Moor Street and ran through the same procedure in reverse, working an all stations stopping train to Liverpool (Lime Street). This was a long and tedious journey, involving calling at some eighteen stations before running down the cutting to Lime Street. Here again I would disconnect the engine, wait until our train was drawn off us then run light engine to Edge Hill Shed, back up the dirty cutting. Once on the shed I would dislodge clinker, formed during our morning's work, then lift it out of the firebox with the long-handled paddle and deposit it on the ground; no mean feat on an engine with an umbrella cab covering the whole of the footplate. Afterwards it was to the water-column, to top up the tank for the third time that morning, then coal her to capacity and run into Downhill Sidings to work a 'run' of empty coaches to Liverpool (Lime Street). Our last duty was to back on our own train and work the 12.05p.m. stopping train to Warrington (Low Level), to be relieved at 1.08p.m., — the end of a hard day's graft. Surely the nickname of it being a nose bag job was more than justified, and it was whilst finishing off this duty that we were to go to weekend camp.

Hurrying home I bolted down my dinner, had a stand up bath (I had no time for a proper one) before changing into khaki uniform and then rushing away to Arpley Station, to be picked up by Army trucks which would take us to Thelwall. We had previously been detailed as to what equipment we were to carry, and when we were well on the road to camp, I realised with a sickening dread that, in my haste, I had forgotten my steel helmet. Too late now, I thought, but what was I going to do?.

Arriving at Greenfields, we marched in ranks to the parade ground which was, in fact, a large meadow. On arrival there we joined a large contingent of regular Army soldiers, who were already neatly lined up in crack formation. The adjutant of this full battalion bawled out orders, telling us we were now under the jurisdiction of the Crown, with all its dire consequences, and I thought, God! they'll probably shoot me! He then informed us that the inspection by the senior officer would now take place.

I could almost feel his approach and, when he drew near to me, I swear I could see him out of the back of my head. He was now a couple of feet away and I could hear his muffled voice, then he stopped right behind me. What was he thinking, I wondered? There were some 400 men on that parade, all steel-helmeted except for one man sporting a glengarry — me! The ground refused to open and swallow me, as I so earnestly desired, and then the officer was touching the gas mask on my back. Was I hearing rightly? He was actually complimenting me on my spotless gas mask. I suppose he had to say something, but was I glad? I should say so.

After the parade, which seemed endless, we had our evening meal, only to fall in later and start a mock battle. It was the Army versus the Home Guard, as we were now called — racehorses against donkeys! We had visions of a Saturday night out in the nearby 'Pickering Arms' but, alas, the battle lasted until gone 11p.m. By that time we were all dirty and dishevelled and most of us, myself included, were covered in cow dung. We stank! Stripping off our uniforms and tumbling into our bunks, most of us were asleep as soon as our heads touched our overcoats, which acted as pillows. I certainly was, having been out of bed since 3.30a.m. and on the go ever since.

Reveille shattered any dreams we may have been enjoying, and it was a scramble for the few buckets of warm water available; alas we had no chance against experienced old sweats of the regular Army, so we had to settle for cold. It didn't matter too much as it was a mild morning anyway, and the cold water was somewhat stimulating. When we sat down for our breakfast of porridge, bacon and kippers we were delightfully hungry, and wolfed it down with hearty relish. After breakfast, another mock battle took place and one of our sergeants, a powerfully-built goods guard called Jimmy Dyson, managed to break his nose when leading us on a charge of the 'enemy', colliding with an equally hefty sergeant of the Army. I could not help feeling relieved that it was not me he had run into.

Soon we boarded the trucks before being driven back to Arpley Station, to be dismissed in proper military fashion. It was now noon, an ideal time for about half a dozen of us to head straight for the Roe Buck Hotel, and it was here that we enjoyed the wonderful relaxation in the friendly atmosphere of bantering conversation, after the strenuous weekend. Afterwards I walked up the main street with Tommy Atkinson, a fellow fireman who also worked in the 'rack'. Approaching Market Gate, the centre point of the town, two small boys asked us if we had any souvenirs, which amused Tommy immensely; he said they must think we are Dunkirk heroes. By our appearance, this was more than likely. Catching a bus I arrived home and retired to bed, where I slept soundly for the next few hours.

A few weeks later one of our drivers died. As he had been an NCO in our platoon we decided to give him a military funeral, to be attended by volunteers. I put my name on the list of privates who would march behind the cortège, and in order that I would be available on the afternoon of the funeral, I had to ask for special privilege to book on at a later time. As I had a paper time for 12 noon I was allowed to 'stand back' until 7p.m., although this meant that I would automatically be on a late shift for the rest of the week.

The time of the funeral arrived, and our lads were immaculately turned out in smart uniforms with boots polished and buttons shining. The coffin was draped with the Union Flag and, in true military bearing, we marched behind in unison; in step and with neat precision. Having due respect and sympathy for our dead comrade, the whole procedure was a credit to the railwaymen who made up the 78th South Lancs., West Lancashire Division. Although the occasion was one of solemnity tinged with a degree of sadness I was, nevertheless, proud to have taken part.

All in all we had our good times and sometimes we roughed it, and although many comedians have since used the Home Guard as the butt of their humorous witticisms, we were to have been the last obstacle of defence if Hitler's army had succeeded in their threatened invasion, and I'm quite sure we would have fought to the last man. After the end of the war I was fortunate to be awarded the Defence Medal.

CHAPTER FIVE

Rough Trips

Arriving at the shed at 12.45p.m. one Monday, the RSF asked me to work to Carlisle. This entailed 'double-trip' working, booking off at the destination, lodging, taking the minimum rest period of nine hours and then working back to our home station. Normally we would have been advised to come prepared, by bringing enough food for the extended length of time we would be away from home, but today we weren't. This was because the Control, for some reason, had not been informed of this train until it was in the area. In order to augment the meagre few sandwiches I had brought with me for a single turn, the RSF obtained a tin of peas, a tin of beans and a packet of biscuits from a cupboard in the Shed Master's office. This was stocked with food for emergencies such as this, and was specifically to subsidise a man's lawful rations.

We relieved the Llandudno men, who had worked the train from their home station, and then set off northwards. Due to traffic on the railways being at saturation point, it was impossible to have a clear road for any considerable distance and, consequently, when we arrived at Carnforth, our eight hours had already expired, and we ourselves now needed to be relieved. From here we travelled as passengers to Preston, in order to lodge in the hostel there, there being none at Carnforth.

After a good wash in this establishment, I ate the tin of peas I had been issued with earlier at Warrington. It does not need much imagination to visualise just how lacking in relish these were without bread, and not even a drink of any kind to help wash them down. Eight hours later, at 5.30a.m., the hostel steward knocked on the door of my cubicle and told me to book on at 6.30a.m. So for breakfast I had the beans, nothing else.

We made our way to Preston Shed, to be told to walk to the station and relieve a train for Crewe. Whilst waiting for this train to arrive we went into the Forces' canteen, where we were given a most welcome cup of tea which we enjoyed immensely. This oasis of refreshment was essentially for the armed forces, but the hand of hospitality was extended to trainmen as they often worked long hours, all too frequently on empty stomachs. Fortunately, only a few locomen abused this privilege. Upon leaving we were politely given two small sandwiches, and to show our appreciation we placed a donation in the box provided.

Our train arrived, headed by Midland Class 4F No. 4406, foolishly called a 'Standard'. The amount of coal which had been used was noticeable, as the train had only come from Barrow, and we thought it strange; we were not long in finding out, for as we set off over the bridge spanning the Ribble, no distance at all from the station we had just left, the needle of the steam-gauge was already going the wrong way — down instead of up.

After struggling against adverse conditions, fighting for steam and jeopardising the boiler in order to gain a few pounds on the clock, this being on an uphill gradient, we staggered on to Euxton. Here we were hopelessly 'down the nick', and my driver had no alternative but to stop for a 'blow up'. I sprinkled coal round the box and wound the blower open to its full extent, but it was clear that she wasn't responding, even though we were standing still. Gaining a few pounds on the gauge I put the injector to work, and back went the pressure. Next I inspected the fire; it was dirty, full of ash and clinkered. I got hold of the dart from the tender, but trying to dislodge the clinker was like trying to break concrete; it was solid. I heaved and pushed but only succeeded in penetrating the ash, the clinker refusing to budge. It was hopeless, so we crawled our way up the long steep incline to the top of Coppull, which seemed to be at the other end the world; we made it, but not without two more stops in order to maintain a safe level of water in the boiler.

As we passed Bank Top Cottages I breathed a sigh of relief, although I knew it was only a brief respite. From here the road was downhill to Standish where we were turned out of the way over the Whelley Line, thus avoiding Wigan. This line was like the Big Dipper on Blackpool Pleasure Beach. It dropped down gradients only to rear up again over little summits, then down into valleys and up steep banks once more, all the way to Bamfurlong. It took us an extremely long time to traverse this stretch, flogging the life out of the boiler going uphill, then coaxing her to allow some water to be taken into her boiler whilst coasting downhill. Alas, it was a battle that we were doomed to lose from the start, and when we arrived at Bamfurlong I had to walk to the signalman to inform him that we could not proceed in our dilapidated condition.

Back on the footplate, I prepared myself for the unthankful task ahead. Before I could do anything at all I had to bale out paddleful after paddleful of fire until, eventually, I made some room inside the firebox to work. Moving as much fire as I could to one side, I managed to dig down to the bars on one side, which were covered by clinker. Delving robustly into this with the dart, I finally managed to break it, although the dart was bent like a shepherd's crook with the exertions that had been placed on it. Occasionally I would throw the dart to the ground, then climb down and place it between the spoke of the engine wheel to press it back into a more employable shape.

I worked on that fire for something like an hour and a half; by this time the grate had cooled considerably, and the fruits of my labours were evident by the huge pile of ashes at the side of the track. The job now was to warm her up, so I spread coal on the grate, little by little, thus giving it time to ignite. When we were ready to leave I walked to the signal box to inform the 'bobby', and then we were out on the main line climbing the bank past Cross Tetleys. Even now, with a comparatively clean fire, she did not respond, and the needle refused to stay on the red line on the gauge. But with coaxing and persuasion we managed, and soon we were in the Warrington area. I had endured a gruelling day up to now, and if a relief had climbed aboard I would have been exceedingly glad. But as it was only about 1p.m., my driver did not want relieving, as this would make us available for duty in the early hours of the morning. So once again we sallied forth, plodding laboriously up the rising gradient at Acton Grange which climbed over the Manchester Ship Canal. Reaching the big iron bridge, which marked the county boundary of Lancashire and Cheshire, the road declined slightly to Moore, so my driver tried to exploit this easy descent by easing the regulator, using the weight of the train to run us down to the troughs which were placed on the level stretch at Moore.

I wound down the scoop and managed to fill the tank, thus relieving ourselves of worries regarding water. From here the level road stretched to Norton Crossing, the start of an uphill climb to Birdswood. The regulator had to be opened and the engine pounded to negotiate this bank, but we still approached the top with the water far too low for comfort and the steam well below the full pressure. As we passed the box, my mate shouted to the 'bobby' to put us 'inside', as we could not continue without serious attention to the fire and boiler.

Once clear of the main line we were free to attend to the urgent needs of our steam-shy engine, and the next forty minutes were spent putting some life into the fire, with the dart, pricker and paddle being used diligently. When we had improved our position slightly, with the fire burning a little more freely and the water half an inch from the 'top nut' of the gauge glass, I walked to the 'bobby' and told him we were ready to leave.

The road from here was fairly level, but as we ran over the River Weaver Viaduct our Class 4F locomotive was struggling to haul her train, due to her inadequate poundage. We had another three miles to cover before we could once again be turned out of the way, at Acton Bridge, to ease on down the slow line to Hartford. Arriving at the home signal I again had to inform the signalman that we would require some time to recuperate, although half an hour later I was on my way to advise him we were ready. Thus it was with a full head of steam, and with the water well up the glass, that we travelled up the main line to Verdin's, some six miles to the south. That short distance took its toll, and yet again we were forced to take refuge in the loop here. Again the minutes ticked by as we coaxed her to raise some steam for the next sprint, which would take us to the slow line at Winsford.

By now I was very tired with the exertions of the day, and was famished for the want of food, but most of all I was desperately in need of a drink; my mouth was so dry that I knew it was hopeless to attempt to eat the biscuits I still had. So it was on to Winsford where we turned down the slow line, along which we plodded to Minshull Vernon only to stop for another blow up, then through Coppenhall to the coal yard. Here we were detained by signals, to await a passage on to the sidings at Basford Hall, and although it was a welcome rest in one sense, by now I was sick, weary and tired of this ugly 'plus four', and longed to be rid of her and on my way home. We finally crawled on to the sidings, where I hooked her off the train and took her on to Crewe South Shed. The fire was, by now, 'up to the arch', (an exaggerated term used to indicate a terribly dirty fire) but in this case it was no exaggeration as it was literally right up to the brick arch, and the amount of coal remaining on the tender was hardly enough to fill a gardener's wheelbarrow. Screwing on the handbrake, and collecting our personal belongings, we made our way to the station to catch the 5.30p.m. express to Warrington.

This train was, as usual, running late, and after a quick run, which took about half an hour, we finished at Dallam at 7.10p.m. My mother was relieved to see me — she had obviously been worried, and soon made me a hearty meal which I devoured, but it was not long before I was tucking into yet another plateful of food. Very soon, I was in the 'Land of Nod'.

Maiden Trip, Carlisle

It was January 1942, and even though I had gained some main line experience I was still only nineteen years of age. As yet, the furthest north I had been was Carnforth, but one wintry Saturday night I was called to book on at 8.10p.m. for a 'double-trip' to Carlisle. With a small attaché case packed with food, I asked for my time card, and ascertained the number of our locomotive. It was No. 9095, a 'Super D', with the smokebox bearing the code 10C (Patricroft). I was somewhat disappointed at this, as I would have much preferred a 'Black Five'.

The engine had already been prepared for us, so we were due off the shed at 8.25p.m. to run to Froghall where we backed on to our train for Carlisle. The train was an express freight, having one third of the vehicles fitted with the continuous vacuum-brake. I coupled the shackle and vacuum-pipes and put the headlamps in their proper position on the smokebox, one on the top bracket under the chimney and the other on the right-hand buffer; this code of 'top and right' indicating a 'crack' train — one that was timed to a fast schedule. My mate then blew up and obtained the required 21in. on the vacuum-gauge, and soon we were under way.

From Froghall we were turned out on to the fast line, with all the signals in the 'clear' position; we were 'right away', but as we passed Winwick Junction it became apparent that the engine was not steaming too well at all. I shut off the injector, hoping she would make a few pounds on the clock, but this action was done only with reluctance, as an engine does not steam so well on low water. Then, when the injector was used to fill up the boiler, the pressure suffered and before reaching Golborne Junction we were in dire straits. The pressure had dropped considerably, and as a good head of steam was necessary to maintain 21in. of vacuum this, in consequence, also suffered with the gauge registering only 15in.

We were now caught up in a vicious circle. This dropping of the vacuum had the same effect as if the driver had indeed applied the brake, so not only were we short of steam to haul the train, but we now had brakes dragging on, thus making the train heavier to pull. I fought hard to raise a few precious pounds, in order to put the injector to work to keep some water showing in the glass, but it was a battle I was losing and, after a terrific struggle against worsening odds, we topped the summit at Coppull. It was down bank from here, and I made the best of this respite to force her to gain some steam and raise the water up the glass. Whilst coasting down this incline I opened the firehole door and looked at the fire; it was a yellowish off-white, a healthy sign indicating that the fire was clean and burning properly. It was then I found she had no brick arch and, on further inspection, that the tube plate was clogged with soot. This soot, incidentally, would harden like solid rock, thus depriving the boiler water of vital heat. There was nothing I could do about this, and it was a sobering thought that I had another hundred miles to go on this 'cripple'.

We rolled down to Preston, hardly needing any steam for the ten mile descent from Coppull. By this time I had the boiler as high as I dared, for these engines were prone to priming due to the low altitude of the boiler. I had a full head of steam and the fire was clean and white-hot, but I knew this state would not last long when the regulator was opened. Leaving Preston Station the road climbed steeply, albeit for a short distance, and she had to be flogged accordingly. The pressure had fallen noticeably, and when we passed St. Wernbergh's Church we were under pressure and struggling.

Going over the troughs at Brock, I lowered the dip, and as my attention was diverted by the injector not working properly, I left the dip in the troughs too long. I paid for this oversight with a pair of wet shoes and socks, as the water cascaded down the well of the tender, bringing with it an avalanche of coal. I took good care not to repeat this action when going over Hest Bank Troughs, raising the dip in good time here, but when I looked out my heart sank because the distant signal for Carnforth was in the 'clear' position. Even though I had never been past this point I knew, from other men, that the road from here climbed steadily for some thirty miles. It rose sharply to Burton Holme so I did everything I could to coaxe her to raise a few pounds, but as soon as I put the injector to work the steam pressure paid forfeit. Reaching this point, however, the gradient eased; not downhill, but at a lesser incline. This stretch was not a great distance and, on passing Milnthorpe, the gradient rose again, heavier than ever. Up this all-exhausting bank No. 9095 simply plodded, and the road uphill seemed endless. Eventually we wheezed our train into the loop at Oxenholme, and it was here we had to pull her round to a more capable position in which to tackle the heavier gradient ahead.

From Oxenholme a bank engine was provided, to assist us on our forlorn journey. Our own engine had to be flogged as we punished her up through Hay Fell and over the viaduct at Lambrigge, to our next haven of refuge at Grayrigg. Again, when we were clear of the main line, I tried to bring her to a full head of steam and a full glass but then we were away again, on what would normally have been an easy run along the level stretch to Tebay. By now I was physically tired, and longing for rest. When we arrived at this hamlet, set in the heart of the mountains, I detached the engine because the tender was 'swept out', with not even a couple of hundred weight of coal left. Therefore we took her on shed, to have her coaled, and while this was being carried out I tried in vain to scrape her tubeplate with an enormously long-handled rake. It was hopeless, so I gave up.

Hooking on to our train again we steamed gently out of the loop to Tebay North, to wait for the tell-tale two 'crows' which heralded the bank engine in position at the rear — at least we would have some assistance up the 7¾ mile sheer climb of Shap. After a long tedious struggle we made it to Shap Summit, but not without a stop for a blow up at Scout Green, half-way up that murderous incline. But make it we did, and it was a heartening thought to know it was downhill for the last thirty miles. We finished at Carlisle at 2.50p.m. Sunday afternoon, after having been on duty for eighteen hours and forty minutes. Taking rest in the hostel, we booked on duty at 1a.m. to work back home and finished at Dallam at 2.30p.m. Monday afternoon, completing my maiden trip to Carlisle.

At 2p.m. Sunday afternoon, I had just started my shift 'outside turning'. My mate was Tommy Buxworth, and our job was to marshal the engines in the order they were due off the shed as from midnight. First of all we inspected the shed — it was absolutely packed with engines, so it was difficult to know where to start. Climbing aboard the one nearest to the 'free end' of the shed, we saw that it had very little steam, something like 40lb. This was just enough to move it, although it would have to be done carefully, so the first move was to release the handbrake, although this was easier said than done.

When a handbrake has been applied with the engine high in steam, it can only be taken off by equalising the pressure on the handgear by the application of the steam-brake. It was then easy to release but now, however, we had no such power, and the only way it could be taken off was to hammer it with a coal pick. Unfortunately, the tools were kept in the stores, so I had to traipse down to the bottom of the shed, where the stores were situated, to retrieve this implement of release. Having done this, my mate opened the regulator and moved over the points which led to the coal stage then, when I turned them, reversed the locomotive into the coal hole. Setting the engine alongside the wagon, from which the coal would be thrown, by a man with a square-bladed shovel, I inspected the fire. It had been cleaned and was burning well, so I threw a few lumps of coal on by hand to keep it warm. We then walked to the top of the shed again, to repeat the performance with another engine, this time one that was 'engine north' so that when it was placed against the one already in the coal hole, which was 'engine south', the two tenders would be together thus enabling two coalmen to work at the same time. When they were ready, we had the difficult task of returning them to an adjacent road in order to put two more in the 'hole'. Whilst the coalmen were busily employed on these two, my mate and I shuffled several engines in order to make room to stable the ones that had been dealt with.

This was the nature of our work; moving engines that had little or no steam. Those that were 'dead' had to be hauled, and to do this I had to throw the shackle over the hook, an acrobatic feat when standing in a pit with the hook about 8ft. above. Once the shackle was thrown upwards and forwards it could be disastrous to miss the hook, because then the shackle would come hurtling down and the unfortunate victim in the pit would receive a nasty blow, possibly serious injury.

There were ten roads on the shed itself, with two on the east side and two on the west, in addition to the coal stack siding, the turntable road and the pit road alongside the coal stage. We placed three dead engines in the stack sidings, a long, hard and tedious job, hooking them on one at a time and dragging them at a snail's pace over the far points, then pushing them back laboriously to secure them by the handbrake, finally diving underneath to unhook the shackle. The table road extended beyond the turntable for one engine-length, and when we had turned the 6a.m. Carlisle engine, we placed her beyond the table to provide us, at least temporarily, with some extra room. The 8.30a.m. Middlewich locomotive also required turning, and we left this on the table after facing her in the right direction.

The job of turning was no simple operation. Normally, when the engine had a good head of steam, the vacuum-pipe was attached to the turntable motor and then, with both ejectors open on the footplate, the table was moved round by vacuum-power. In effect, the engine turned itself. Alas, when there was insufficient steam to blow the required vacuum, the table had to be manhandled by the double-handled apparatus. This took the combined efforts of two men, who invariably had to stop a couple of times to regain their breath.

From the table itself, to the point of clearance on the ajoining shed road, there was enough room to accommodate one engine, so we left one there for the time being. Thus we had engines all over the place, and to make matters worse the shed staff (steam raisers and firedroppers) took care of the engines that were on the shed roads only, and not those that were on roads outside the shed. Therefore I had the added responsibility of keeping my eye on those that were not on shed. Once we had a few coaled up and berthed, we could then 'build up' on the engines that we would not be handling again.

After about 3½ hours steady slogging, we put two more locomotives in the coal hole, which required quite a substantial amount of coal, and would take some considerable time for the men to deal with. This was a cunning manoeuvre, as we could now partake of our sandwiches. We had barely finished our evening snack when there was a bellowing from the coal bench; the coalmen had done their work on the two engines, and now wanted a couple more; I may state here that the men were paid on a piece-rate. Once again we were busily engaged in moving, berthing and then making room inside the shed for engines that were not on a shed road so that they, too, could be placed either in the shed or outside, so long as they were on a shed road. Around 9.30p.m., after a hard day's work, we washed our hands in a bucket of warm water and retired to 'Annie's' for a pint — which we justly deserved.

On a lovely Monday in the month of May, I had an availability paper for 12 noon. I had just had lunch, and was eagerly awaiting the knock of the call boy summoning me to work, because on such a beautiful day as this it would be a pleasure to have a trip out of town. The minutes ticked by, but there was no knock and eventually an hour passed, then another, and still I waited. The clock ticked away the afternoon and tea-time came; as I waited I had my tea. It was getting cooler now, with the sun going down. Evening came, and there was still no sound on the door knocker. By 7p.m. the lovely day had passed, and I had not savoured its benefits the way I would have liked. By 8p.m. I was tired of waiting and indeed, the prospect of going to work now did not appeal to me at all. Just before 9p.m. I answered the door to the call boy, who informed me that I was to book on at 9.55p.m., as required. I felt bitter and more than a little disgusted; I had been called five minutes short of the maximum ten hours from paper time, but worse was to come. When I reported to the RSF at 9.55p.m. he told me to go 'steam-raising', a task normally performed by shedmen but, due to the wartime manpower shortage, it had been agreed by the unions that firemen could be utilised for this duty.

The job, in simple terms, was to build up the fire after it had been dropped by the 'firedroppers'. It involved raising the steam to a low pressure while, at the same time, keeping the engine warm in readiness for the fireman to raise the poundage, just before the scheduled time off the depot. A simple enough job on the face of it, but it meant climbing numerous handrails to attend to a large number of engines in the care of the 'steamraiser'. The next step was to spread the small amount of fire left in by the 'fire-droppers' with the paddle, then shovel enough coal on to the grate so that the fire would grow yet, at the same time, not create too much steam. The 'steamraiser' would also keep the boiler some three-parts full. After climbing down the steps of one engine, he had to repeat the action on the next; truly a tiring activity. There were two 'steamraisers' on the night shift but, as there were fifty plus engines on the shed at night, it was no job for a weakling.

I opted for roads Nos. 1-5, the other five roads being in the charge of the regular man. I worked diligently, going round each engine in my care, topping up the boilers and ensuring there was enough coal on their fires to keep them warm, yet not so little that it would burn away. When I finished my first excursion it was after 1a.m., so I took this opportunity to eat my late meal. I could not afford to dawdle over this, as the first engine I had attended to would now require further attention; also, if I had lingered in the cabin I would surely have fallen asleep.

With a shovel on my shoulder and a gauge lamp in my hand, I went about my business. I had administered care to a large number of engines when I came to an L&YR Class 3F, which needed a good deal of water in the boiler, so I put the injector to work and sat down for a rest whilst the boiler was filling up. Alas! The long wait of the previous day and the dark, early hours of the morning had taken their toll; I fell asleep. I have no idea just how long I dozed, but I awoke feeling frozen and with a crick in my neck; I had slept whilst sitting on the sandbox, made of good old-fashioned steel. The injector was still singing merrily, and I immediately turned it off. It was a known fact that 'Lanky' injectors worked better when the pressure was low; it was low now, but how the boiler was I had no way of knowing. I then tried the water gauge cocks — the glass filled up immediately the cocks were closed, so to say the boiler was full would be a gross understatement; it must have been up to the safety-valve. Therefore I opened the small ejector, left it open, and climbed off the footplate. This action would waste water up the chimney.

On a point of interest concerning the ex-L&YR 0-6-0 engine (3F), there were six types which were designated '3F' by the LMS, and numbered, prior to nationalisation, 12083-435, 12436-60, 12461-7, 12515-36, 12537-56 and 12557-619. The first type had the Aspinall round-topped boiler, but some had been given Belpaire boilers before entering LMS ownership. The second batch was the Hughes type, identical to the original Aspinall. The third series from No. 12436 was not built until 1917/18, and were also Hughes-designed, but none were built with saturated Belpaire boilers. Hughes, again, designed batches four and five, and both had their notable differences but the final batch from No. 12557 was allocated these numbers after being rebuilt with superheaters. Most originally had Aspinall round-topped boilers, but some were from the Hughes-built saturated batch.

I told the 'outside turner' the plight of this locomotive, as it would be dangerous to move it in its present state. If the regulator was opened in the normal manner, the regulator valve would draw water into the cylinders and could quite easily result in the cylinder ends being knocked out, thus constituting an obvious danger to anyone in the vicinity. If, however, the cylinder ends held, the engine would be difficult, if not impossible, to stop, as the power driving it would be hydraulic. The 'outside driver' thanked me for telling him. I had to remember that I had left that small ejector open because if I forgot, the boiler would eventually empty itself, thus endangering the fusible plug.

As daylight dawned, at about 5a.m., I didn't feel as tired and kept an eye on that boiler. The ejector had blown for nearly an hour, and when the cocks were tested the water did not flood the glass when the cocks were closed, this proved the boiler was now low enough not to be dangerous. After another quick round of the engines I was ready to call it a day, so I washed my hands and prepared for home. Trudging homewards, I reflected what a rotten lousy occupation I had chosen for my career.

CHAPTER SIX

Accidents

One Thursday night in November, I arrived at the shed to start my night's work. We were to work the 11.45p.m. service to Birmingham, for which an engine was already prepared, so we took the train to Crewe, where we were relieved, then walked to the South Shed to prepare two locomotives for other engine crews, and afterwards, we worked the 5.55a.m. slow goods to Froghall.

Nothing out of the ordinary happened on the outward journey; we did our job, and had our supper whilst on shed at Crewe. Backing on to our train for the return trip we found we had 66 wagons, containing mostly coal, and none fitted with vacuum-brake. We reached Birdswood, where the road descended to Norton Crossing and levelled out; to work a train successfully over this stretch meant keeping the couplings tight by allowing a breath of steam to the cylinders. Then, when the bottom of the decline was reached, a little more steam was needed to drag the train beneath the overhead canal bridge which marked the bottom of the bank. It was almost impossible to take the train through here without receiving a 'pluck' from the rear, as the engine passed the box at Norton Crossing. A conscientious fireman always looked back here to make sure the train was still intact.

Coming past the box on this particular morning, we felt the inevitable 'pluck', but I also heard a sound something like the 'ping' one hears when a gun has been fired. Smoke was battening down on to our footplate, because the gentle exhaust from the cylinders was not raising it. I could not see anything because of the smoke, so I hit the blower handle hard with my hand. This lifted the smoke and, peering through the darkness, I could make out a shocking situation. The engine had come adrift from the train and we were running light, while following us at a brisk rate were 66 wagons over which we had no control. We were traversing a right-hand bend, so my driver could not possibly see our predicament. He was a good engineman and a careful driver, but he was not a young man, so I anticipated his next move when I walked across the footplate. Before I told him anything I placed my hand on the vacuum-controlled steam brake. He did as I had expected; he made towards the brake as I informed him of our circumstances, but my hand prevented him from touching it. Had he touched that brake, there would have been a terrible calamity, with us in the thick of it.

'Let her run, Jim', I said, 'and when they are close I'll shout to you, then we can stop them.'

I watched and waited, and it went through my mind what that famous General said to his soldiers about not firing until they could see the whites of the enemy's eyes. It was a sight I shall never forget, a runaway train hurtling along, and us right in its path. Still I waited, because I knew I had to time it exactly. When the wagons were a couple of feet from us I shouted 'Right, Jim!'; I wanted him to give her a bit of steam but alas, instead of opening the regulator a touch he grabbed the brake. With a terrific thud they hit us, and we were knocked forward at an accelerating pace before the brake started to grip. When I looked back all I could see from the point of impact was a great black cloud of coal dust, absolutely enveloping us and the train while obscuring my vision completely. I shouted to my mate to hold the wagons at all costs, so he kept the brake hard on, but it seemed ages before we eventually slithered to a stand at the south end of the troughs.

Before we came to a halt, I was busy opening the detonator cannister. They were usually difficult to open, and the lid had to be prised off. I managed to remove the lid, then, stuffing the detonators in my pockets, I jumped from the engine as soon as we stopped. Looking back along the 'up' line I saw a green colour light; it was the distant signal for Norton Crossing, and my heart sank. I set off in a tremendous hurry, but did not get far before I fell flat on my back. The water which had spilled over the troughs had frozen; forming a surface similar to a skating rink. Hastily I got to my feet and sped towards Acton Grange. A train was headed in my direction but, fortunately, dawn was breaking so the driver saw my red flag and quickly brought his train under control. I informed him of the circumstances, and then proceeded to the box to enlighten the 'bobby'.

Afterwards, I walked back to our engine to see what damage had been done. The leading vehicle and our locomotive were buffer-locked, while the second one had forced its buffers through the ½in. thick steel of the wagon preceding it. The rear wheels of this were about 1ft. above rail level, together with the leading pair of the second one. I examined the damage; it was plainly obvious what had happened by the broken link hanging from the engine drawbar hook. Despite this our train was, fortunately, not fouling the opposite running line. I gave this information to the signalman, later, when I returned to his box, and he assured me he would stop all subsequent trains and warn their drivers to proceed past our hapless train with great caution.

At 11.30a.m. a passenger train stopped alongside us, to enable a set of men to alight. They were our relief, and, as they walked the short distance to our engine, the driver slipped on the icy boards in between the sleepers under the troughs. He fell flat on his back, as I had done earlier. As for us, we walked to Acton Grange and eventually procured a ride down to Arpley on the bank engine.

One day, in the glorious month of June, I was firing the 8.25a.m. Walton Old Junction to Bamfurlong service; a local job on which we did a good deal of shunting at wayside goods yard on the way to Bamfurlong. As we were going only about ten miles to our destination, we always travelled in a tender first direction on the outward journey, as it was not practicable to turn at this yard. It also enabled the driver to be on the same side as the shunter, when we reached Winwick Quay on our return trip.

We were late leaving Walton, which was not unusual, and made our way along the 'down' slow line, and upon reaching Winwick Quay we almost came to a stand at the signals, but just as we reached them the 'calling on' arm was lowered for us. This indicated that the section between the Quay and the Junction was occupied, so we could proceed only a far as the line was clear; all perfectly legitimate, and within regulations. It was quite normal to find a train in front at this location, and drivers were aware of this. On this particular occasion, however, my driver was not prepared to find five in front, but this was the case and, due to being tender first, his view was impaired by the large tender of our Class 8F locomotive.

As my mate opened the regulator to accelerate, I bent down to tidy the footplate, and the next few minutes were chaotic. The oil bottle shot out of the tool cupboard, to the right of the boiler, and hit me squarely on the backside while simultaneously, the bucket of spanners fell from the shelf above the handbrake, and hit me plumb on the head. I immediately stopped what I was doing, and looked out from the cab to see what had happened. In front of us was the brake van of the train in front, and even as I watched, in fascinated amazement, a wagon, two in front of the brake van, mounted the one in front of it. It looked as if this wagon was trying to climb on to the other and indeed, that is precisely where it finished its crazy, acrobatic feat, on top of the other. There was no time to lose; one glance on the fast line side of the footplate told its own story. The wagons were in anything but an orderly straight line as they should have been — they were in a zigzag fashion, and what was of vital importance, they were foul of the fast line. I did not hesitate for a second. It was imperative that the fast line should be protected, and even though it was the duty of the guard to carry out this vital operation, I realised that time was the element I had to overcome. Grabbing the detonator cannister I prised off the lid and, stuffing the red flag in my pocket, I slid, rather than climbed, down the handrails. I was away like a shot.

As I ran in the fast line 'four foot', in the direction from which a train would approach, my heart sank. The 'down' fast home was in the 'clear' position, but what was more frightening, the train was already on its way. My blood froze, but I ran forward, frantically waving the red flag. I thought the driver was never going to see it but, after what seemed like an age, a cloud of smoke billowed from his chimney, a tell-tale sign that the driver had shut off steam. Then I heard a wonderful sound, the metallic screech of brakes. There was no need to run now, so I walked to the engine and climbed aboard, informing the driver of the circumstances and asking him to await further instruction. I then went to the box, to acquaint the signalman with the dangerous situation.

This, then, effected complete protection, my errand of mercy fulfilled. My thighs suddenly felt like water, my legs not supporting my body, so I sat down, involuntarily. The 'bobby' gave me a drink of water and, within a few minutes, I was recovered. I suppose it was a natural reaction after that hell-fire dash along the track, coupled with the anxiety of wondering whether I was going to succeed. I then went to view the condition of the train we had hit. Overhanging the fast line was a steel wagon, the corner of which was protruding into a space perpendicular to the left running rail. The train I had mercifully stopped was a schoolchildren's special, bound for Blackpool. The dangerously protruding corner was exactly at the height and angle to act as a guillotine to slice hundreds of little heads from tender young bodies, as they looked innocently out of the windows. Thank heaven the terrible calculation did not materialise into a macabre disaster.

I felt justly proud that I had diverted the horrible path of mutilation, and firmly expected a letter of commendation from the powers that be. Alas, I was disappointed, no such letter was received! However, I feel that had my superiors witnessed the accident, and, like I, seen the possible terrible consequences that could have followed, they would have thanked me for my efforts in avoiding this possible tragedy.

CHAPTER SEVEN

The Haydock Colliery Branch

One of our jobs, the 8.44a.m. Dallam to Haydock working, was, apart from the serious side of our work, little short of hilarious. We would start from the Dallam Branch with a train of coal empties destined for Haydock Colliery, situated just about a mile north of Earlestown. It was as we left Earlestown that the fun started.

Here we crossed the main line at a right angle, and immediately encountered a short steep rise between rows of houses. Surmounting this little knoll we would stop because here, the railroad dipped towards a highway guarded by crossing gates. These were operated by a man in a cabin belonging to the colliery, as indeed, from Earlestown, the whole ramshackle railway was colliery property. Protecting this level crossing was a signal made simply of wood, and in no way could this be described as an advertisement for gloss paint; it was more like a piece of planking from one of the coal wagons. From the crossing, the rail road climbed abruptly almost to the pithead. We waited on top of the first incline for two reasons; firstly because we would have difficulty in stopping at the signal and secondly, but most importantly, because we wanted to gain acceleration on the 'down' grade to storm the steep rise beyond. The man controlling the gates would, when the road to the top was clear, come and open the gates by hand, then pull the signal to its 'clear' position. When the signal dropped off we would give steam to the cylinders and start away as quickly as possible, piling on more steam until the regulator was fully open and, in addition, with the second regulator open to its full extent. The engine would emit a tremendous din from the chimney, with steam rising to colossal heights, and the big ends threatening to come through the boiler. The locomotive kept up this Herculean struggle until she came to a little footbridge spanning the railway, where the track levelled out at the top. My mate would then ease her down, and bring the train to a stand just short of the colliery sidings. Here I would hook off the engine, and we would drift into the road which held our wagons for the return trip. It was a stiff drag out of these roads, and in order to back on to the complete train we had to drag half of it and place it on another road before we went back for the other half, to drag this out and then back on the first half, thus making the train complete. It was impossible to drag the whole train out at one go, this simply being too heavy for the engine.

When we were ready to leave, we struggled to haul the coal-laden wagons to the little overbridge, stopping here as we did on the upward journey. The signal box, to flatter this cabin, was now some 200 yards ahead of us and, similar to the opposite direction, a signal controlled our passage. To attempt a descent without the signal being 'clear' would have, indeed, courted disaster; no way would we have been able to stop. When it was lowered we crept on at a snail's pace, moving a spoke's width at a time until suddenly, the train would take over. It started to push us at this point, and that was our cue to wind on the handbrake. Proceeding at a snail's pace, the engine would creep down the steeply falling gradient until about eight or ten wagons were on the slope then, with a suddenness which would have scared anyone not acquainted with this Fred Carno's set-up, the train would lurch forward and gather speed at a frightening rate. From this point we were literally out of control, heading downhill with some thirty odd fully laden coal wagons pushing us past the signal at the level crossing where the line rose slightly to the little knoll, when once again it dipped slightly towards Earlestown.

A few feet in front of the crossing signal were trap points; hence the obvious reason why we waited at the top of the hill for the signal to be lowered. Before the man in the box could lower the signal, the crossing gates had to open to the railway with the traps being set in the correct position. When the gates were open for us they were, of course, closed to the highway, and as this road was rather a busy one, the traffic soon accumulated. It must have been frustrating for the motorists to find their progess halted by gates, apparently with nothing happening and with the train about a furlong away and not moving, or so it would appear at that distance. They soon gave vent to their feelings by blaring their horns and, when the engine shot past them, to all kinds of unspoken insults.

Before the engine reached the top of the rise (the train would then be in the valley caused by the two gradients), she would be brought to a sudden stand by that part of the train on the 'up' gradient being greater than the portion still coming on the 'down'. When this occurred, as indeed it often did, the people in the traffic hold-up would go frantic, as now it was a titanic struggle for the engine to drag the train up the bank to clear the crossing. The engine would slip like mad and throw sparks high in the air, eventually pulling the train clear to allow the gates to be opened for the hapless motorists, who would go on their way with horns blaring and probably using profane language. On the other hand, when the engine reached the knoll, she had to be slowing down and gaining control of her train, as a pair of trap points was sited directly at the bottom of the next small incline, protecting the main Liverpool to Manchester line; should the locomotive not have gained control when reaching this point, we were fully aware that we would never stop at those omnious trap points.

However, this did not happen often, but when it did there was only one course of action to be taken; the driver would dive from the footplate off one side, the fireman from the other. Then, as fast as possible, both men would drop the handles of the wagon brakes and try desperately to pin them down with the aid of the brake sprags, which we always carried on the engine for such emergencies. We nearly always succeeded in bringing the train to a stand, and only on rare occasions did the locomen fail; but it did happen. The engine then would become derailed at the traps, the rest of the train piling on top of it until the vehicles embedded themselves in the ground, halting the rest; it made a terrible disorder of chaos and took a long time to clear the debris.

One humorous incident that springs to mind was when my driver did not know the route to Haydock, and requested the services of a conductor. As we shot over the crossing, with the train shoving like mad, my mate and I dropped from the footplate and waited for the brake van to pass us. Our guard was of a nervous disposition, and as he passed us we shouted to him that we were running away. Upon seeing us on the ground, he immediately assumed that there was no one on the footplate (he did not know, or had forgotten about the conductor), and jumped clean out of the brake van to the floor. All ended well, however, and although he called us names which were anything but Christian, he eventually saw the funny side, and we all had a good laugh about it later. This, then, was the Haydock Colliery Branch, a little railway with its own codes and peculiarities, and certainly a law unto itself.

CHAPTER EIGHT

The Road to the North

One of our regular jobs was the 6a.m. stopping train to Carlisle. To perform this duty we usually had a 'Royal Scot' but sometimes a 'Black Five' and, on occasions, a 'Princess Royal' class locomotive. The 'Princess Royal' class were excellent and economical engines; once the firebox was well stacked with a good fire they would run for miles without further firing. Unfortunately, on this particular job, when we were timed to call at all the stations along the route, they were unsuitable for this kind of work, as with 6ft. 6in. driving wheels they were rather slow to attain their stride, and only gave their best on long runs. This was a pity, because with the bulk of the weight of the firebox slung over the two small bogies directly under the footplate, the result was a smooth riding engine.

The 'Royal Scot' class, having wheels of 6ft. 9in. diameter with no footplate bogies and a parallel boiler (they were later converted to tapered boiler), made a mockery of smooth running. They rocked and rolled all the time they were at speed and with three cylinders, giving six exhaust beats up the chimney with each revolution, they burned coal in a gluttonous manner. Firing this class was something akin to feeding buns to a zoo elephant; they were insatiable, and it was little wonder that they had earned the discreditable nickname of 'Colliers' Friends'. The fireboxes, unlike those on the 'Princess Royal' class which were square, were long and sloping, and with the brick arch following the downward slope of the grate it resembled the opening to the Mersey Tunnel.

The 'Black Five', a two cylinder engine with 6ft. driving wheels and a sloping box that was not too long, made firing something of a pleasure. They were comparatively quick off the mark when leaving stations, and were quite good runners in between. Being economical on coal, and with the boiler being fed by an exhaust injector, these engines were ideal for this type of train running and were loved by locomen everywhere.

One summer morning we booked on at 4.30a.m. to prepare our engine, leaving the shed at 5.30a.m. to run the short distance from Dallam tender first. We hooked on to our train in the sidings, then drew alongside the back platform, ready to leave on the stroke of 6a.m. Our locomotive was a 'Royal Scot', and as we set off from Warrington, using the slip road from the back platform on to the 'down' fast line, past the shunting yards and warehouse of Froghall and the White Cross Wire Works, with the rolling mills of Dallam Forge looming towards us, I began to shovel coal into the long box. We rounded the 60m.p.h. curve at Dallam and ran past the Longford Wire Co., heading for open country towards Winwick Quay and the junction beyond. Away to the left was Burtonwood, an airbase manned by American personnel.

At Winwick Junction we took the road to the left, and began the easy climb up Vulcan Bank. Some 200 yards from the railway was the little country inn bearing the name of 'Fiddle i' th' Bag', although this name had nothing to do with the violin-type of musical instrument. In fact the 'fiddle' was some sort of wooden contraption, by which a sower spread seeds from a bag slung over his shoulder. We then passed three rows of cottages set in the form of a triangle, with the local inn sitting squarely in the centre. Towering above this tiny settlement was the impressive-looking works of Vulcan Foundry; this, together with the village and inn, derived its name from the Roman God of Fire, son of Jupiter and Juno. It is here that locomotives were made for various parts of the world and, indeed, the works contributed tremendously to the war effort by turning out tanks for the Army. Close by was the Wargrave Memorial Hospital, where many a wounded soldier was nursed back to health.

As we reached the top of the 1 in 75 gradient, we were confronted by an unusual piece of railway contour. The line divided into two quarter circles, both joining the main line just a short distance away, thus forming a triangle. There were two platforms on the 'straight', serving the cities of Liverpool and Manchester, with two more on the west side of this triangle where local trains from Warrington stopped to pick up passengers for St. Helens. Lastly there was the curve station situated on the third 'leg', the one we were now approaching. We came to a stand with our train forming an arc, and I jumped from the footplate in order to see the guard's flag when we were ready to depart. Receiving the 'tip' to go, I climbed aboard and my driver opened the regulator. The large wheels of the 'Royal Scot' protested in screeching resentment, as she found adhesion difficult on the acute bend. Moving only a couple of engine-lengths, however, she found the straight of the main line comparatively easy and was quickly into her stride.

Due to double summer time during the war, the clock was an hour in front of Greenwich Mean Time, and the mid-July sun rose like a big red ball and appeared to sit on the rails right in front of us. We could see, too, how the railway between here and Newton-le-Willows hollowed out, and sagged like the wires stretched on telegraph poles. This was due to subsidence, as we were now on the threshold of the Wigan Coalfield, and the permanent way staff had the never-ending job of building up the ballast with cinders. To use any other kind of material would have been futile, as it sank almost as fast as it was built up.

Passing the recreation ground of Mesnes Park the regulator was closed, to allow the engine to drift into the station. Leaving this well-kept platform, we approached Parkside at 15m.p.h., where we shot away to the north and traversed another quarter of a circle to arrive at Lowton. This tiny village station had the honour of stabling the Royal Train when the Monarch, or any member of the Royal Family, was touring in the vicinity. After picking up two passengers, we were confronted by two signals at Golborne Junction, and were obliged to take the left-hand one (which is for the slow line) as the next two scheduled stops had platforms on the slow line only.

In order to place our train on the platform at Golborne we stopped under the bridge, and no self-respecting fireman would allow the safety-valve to blow off here otherwise the footplate, and indeed the whole engine, would be enveloped in steam. Passing Cross Tetleys and Long Lane, both on a downhill gradient, we saw the large wheel of a pit-cage, the first of many, with the signal boxes taking their names from the collieries they served.

The Bamfurlong stop, with its short wooden platform and an overbridge, was a repetition of the one at Golborne. Between these stations we encountered a speed restriction, which had prevailed for some considerable time, due to subsidence, with the line having to be constantly built up with cinders. We then left Bamfurlong, where the Whelley Line veered away as we headed towards Springs Branch, Wigan. As the line from Liverpool trespassed on to ours at this point, we ran over the Leeds & Liverpool Canal. It is on this mediocre waterway that the famous Wigan Pier is situated, and although many people believe the story to be a myth, a brief walk along the tow-path will dispel any doubts.

Coasting into Wigan we came to a stand at the far end of the platform, where we waited for the station duties to be carried out. My mate held the steam-brake spindle out by means of a cloth, the latter being hooked round the top of the small rod connecting the brake steam-plug and the vacuum-plug. This was to hold the train on the rising gradient, as the train would roll back as vacuum was re-created. Pulling out the steam-plug simply allowed steam to the brake cylinder on the locomotive only, which was immediately released once the plug was drawn back by the vacuum controlling it.

Upon starting away from Wigan, the 'Royal Scot' barked furiously from the front end as she hungrily devoured the large quantity of coal I had spread round her whilst waiting to depart; this because the road was steeply inclined to our next stop of Boar's Head. Reaching this tiny halting place, which took its name from the little country inn close to the bridge high above us, a signal box of the same name was positioned at ground level. At one time, admission was gained by a flight of steps leading up to the entrance, this being practical proof of the actions of subsidence underground. We passed Victoria Colliery and called at Standish, where the Whelley Line, which had traversed almost half-a-circle from Bamfurlong, joined us at this point, having avoided the congestion of the main line through Wigan. The Pennines were clearly visible on that lovely morning which is most unusual, for this area is infamous for its smoggy atmosphere and is usually hidden by a pall of fog and smoke.

At Coppull we collected a number of girls, who were employed at Euxton, and continued downhill to Balshaw Lane and Leyland, where some passengers alighted for the paint factory, and on to Farington which was our last stop before reaching Preston. Running over the iron trellis bridge spanning the River Ribble, we were confronted by a maze of signals. Small gantries carrying two or maybe three signals controlled each road, and there were numerous roads by which trains could enter the station; a driver had to have excellent route knowledge to be able to read these at a glance. Upon leaving the platform at the other end, yet another vast array of signals faced us as my driver sought out the ones we required, as we threaded our way on to the north line, thus avoiding the Blackpool line to the west. As we took a gradual bend, which passed directly under the magnificent spire of St. Werbergh's, it became apparent just how high it really was and, indeed, it is said to be the fourth highest in the land.

Gathering speed on the virtually flat road, we passed mile after mile of poultry farms dotted along the route and sped through Barton & Broughton at a brisk rate. Shutting off the injector, I filled the back corners of the firebox and deposited the occasional shovelful along the sides, for we were now approaching Brock. A stream runs under the line just before we reach the signal box; this is the River Brock, from which the box takes its name, a tiny river that meanders westwards to join the Wyre some five miles away. Moving over to the driver's side of the footplate, I released the chain on the water scoop. Keeping my eyes on the woods looming towards us I began to lower the scoop, slowly at first, then as soon as we were level with the outskirts of the woods I lowered it quickly, for we were now on the troughs. Although they are a quarter of a mile long it takes only twelve or thirteen seconds to clear them, and by watching the gauge on the tender I judged the rate at which the water was entering the tank. When it registered 3,000 gallons I began to wind up the scoop because, due to the enormous pressure of water on the scoop at speed, the muscle-power of both arms had to be exercised and by the time the scoop was clear of the troughs, the tank had the 4,000 gallon capacity. If the scoop remained in the trough, even for a second too long, the water would cascade out of the tender and high into the air, with the passengers in the leading two coaches receiving an unwelcome drenching, that is, if the carriage windows were open. Securing the scoop handle, by means of the chain provided, I hit the blower with the palm of my hand so that we would not get a back-flash when the regulator was closed.

At Garstang where, apart from the 'Kenlis Arms' and a dairy, there seemed to be nothing of note, I occupied myself by stoking the engine in readiness for the run to Lancaster. A 'Black Five' thus stoked would easily complete the distance without further fuel, but I knew from experience that a 'Royal Scot' would require firing again before we reached the next station. With the trees in full foliage, and with the Pennines visible along the eastern skyline, the landscape looked picturesque with no foreign elements to pollute the fragrant atmosphere.

Opening the regulator wide and giving her plenty of 'wheel' my mate let her get into her stride before he 'notched back' the wheel, and we were on our way to Lancaster at an ever-increasing speed. Our engine seemed to relish this thrashing, and roared her approval with a deafening bark from her front end. On a flat road like this she was like a thoroughbred straining at the bit, as she bounded along at top speed. The little church at Scorton, with its diminutive steeple, was like a picture one would expect to find in a fairy-tale book. We had a fleeting glimpse of the River Wyre, with its shallow water rippling over the pebble bottom, as it lazily ambled past the caravans which were permanently positioned on its low banks.

Passing Bay Horse at top speed, we had a fleeting glimpse of the little public house that was neatly camouflaged behind a screen of sycamores from which the pub got its name. In the country lane running parallel with us, a signpost pointed the way to Quernmore (pronounced Quarmer), and it was through this lovely scenery that females accused of witchcraft at Pendle, some twelve or fourteen miles away, were walked on their way to being tried at Lancaster in the seventeenth century. We passed this in a flash and were soon hurtling past the solidly-built stone houses of Galgate, with its solitary road which appears to come from nowhere. As we rounded a bend, the signals for Oubec loomed towards us and the loops, one on each side of the main line and long enough to hold one train, were controlled by a single signal box. When no trains are passing, the only sound that can be heard is the bleating of sheep, the lowing of cattle or perhaps the occasional plaintive cry of a curlew as it wheels overhead. It is indeed a desolate place for the men who operate this lonely outpost. As we raced beneath the mental asylum, located high above us on the left bank, my mate closed the regulator and, as the engine reached Lancaster No. 1 box, she heeled over on the cant of the line to negotiate the downhill bend to Castle Station.

Upon leaving, our train had barely cleared the platform when our locomotive was on the heavy iron bridge spanning the River Lune, and we could see the sandbanks which the low tide had exposed. At other times, the river would be high in flood. An electric line, which linked Green Ayre and Morecambe ran along the north bank, while the trim little station of Ladies Walk could be seen in the near distance. We then skirted a slight bend towards Morecambe South Junction, but did not relax speed as our road was straight ahead. Had we been bound for the holiday resort, our speed would have needed to be checked considerably to negotiate the 10 m.p.h. curve. Our next stop was Hest Bank, a delightful locality on the fringe of the bay. No sooner had we left than I walked across to the water pick-up, for we were now running over another set of troughs. As we had not used much water from the last troughs, it was a matter of putting in the scoop and almost instantly winding it up again. At Bolton-le-Sands about half-a-dozen people alighted, and it was obvious from their rucksacks and camping gear that they were heading for the caravan and camping site situated immediately behind the little station. At precisely 7.59a.m., dead on schedule, we ran into Carnforth.

Having risen at the unearthly hour of 3.30a.m. I was, by now, feeling quite hungry, so taking my sandwiches from the coat box on the tender, I placed them on the oil cupboard which was positioned on the fireman's side, adjacent to the boiler, but low on the footplate. Before I started to eat them, though, I had to ladle a good deal of coal on to the fire because, as many drivers loved to quote to the fireman, this was where the work starts! When I had sufficiently stoked the firebox I took a sandwich from the packet, which I had opened just enough to allow one at a time to be taken, so keeping them free from coal dust as far as possible. I then sat and munched one, with my feet on the damper handles, knowing full well that for the next few miles it would be a matter of filling my mouth, then picking up the shovel and feeding this gluttonous monster, even as I fed the inner-man. Miles further on, when I had consumed my snack, I partook of a long drink from the bottle of tea warming on the screen plate.

I often envied the driver, who could eat his lunch without any physical exertion and, more or less, without interruption. Some drivers, particularly passed firemen, would often let me take over the manipulation of the train while I consumed my 'butties', the other man employing himself in firing the engine. This was because they were of the younger element, and still fit enough to flex their muscles heaving coal into a white-hot fire from a rocking footplate. The driver I was firing for on this occasion, although easy to get along with, was way past his youth, and it would have been sacrilegious to expect him to keep steam in this all-devouring coal burner, especially up the banks which were directly ahead of us.

The road now was noticeably steeper, and the heavy beats of the 'Royal Scot' blasted the exhaust sky-high as we climbed past Yealand. A highway, running underneath us at an oblique angle, marked the boundary of the two counties as we left Lancashire and entered Westmorland. We climbed to Burton & Holme where the gradient, although still uphill, eased a little past the prisoner of war camp towards Milnthorpe. We made a brief stop here, and although there were no passengers to board our train, we did collect a few crates, all of which contained farm produce. As soon as we left this outlandish halt we hit the rising ground and climbed past Hincaster, where the nondescript single line from Arnside unobtrusively joined ours as we continued on through Sedgewick and Natland to Oxenholme. This was a rather big station for a rural district, with a separate platform for trains serving the Windermere line. The landscape in this mountainous terrain was little short of marvellous, with the undulating skyline of the Pennines running along the eastern horizon, as far as the eye could see to the south, where it faded into nothingness down towards Carnforth and stretched northwards, to be lost once again in the numerous hills rising majestically before us. The summer foliage decorated the whole scene with every shade of green, tinted profusely with the yellow of Laburnum, the deep reds of Mountain Ash and the purple hue of heather blending into the abundance of natural colour. The magnificent grandeur seemed bereft of time — ancient, yet ageless.

Climbing Hay Fell, with the western lowlands dropping far below us and the white houses of the neat compact town of Kendall away in the distance, we passed under several solidly-built granite bridges which, perhaps, portrayed the character of the local inhabitants. Tucked behind the buttress of one of these bridges was a cottage with an unusual design; four windows were arranged as if ascending a staircase, one window being slightly higher than its neighbour and the top one almost touching the roof. This is Laverock Bridge House, the road from here leading to Mealbank, about a mile away, and further afield to Patton Hall.

The track then turned sharply to Lambrigge Viaduct, running due east before swinging northwards again towards Mosedale Hall Crossing. At Grayrigg we reached the top of the heavy incline, and although nothing of the village could be seen from here, it lay just behind the hills which encompass this tiny wooden platform. The tombstones in the graveyard of Grayrigg Church tell their own story; the vast majority of the people at rest there dwelt in the area known as Moresdale Hall (spelt differently from the name on the signal box), and almost all lived to the ripe old age of ninety plus. Even the few exceptions were octogenarians. In the porch of the church is a handwoven tapestry, made about 100 years ago.

We had a fruitless stop at Low Gill as no one boarded or alighted from our train, and we passed the junction where the old Midland Railway from Clapham Junction (not to be confused with its London namesake) crossed the viaduct, which is a monument to nineteenth century architecture, before running into ours. Long ago the Midland had running rights over this stretch of line, formerly known as the London & North Western Railway, from Low Gill to Carlisle, for which they had to pay, no doubt. From the junction we sped along the easy level, with a high wall of hills on the left and the bank falling steeply away to a rippling stream far below us on the other. The cool clear waters gurgled and sparkled over half-submerged rocks lying on the pebble bed, as it made its winding way to Lancaster, for this beautiful meandering creek was indeed the River Lune, although a completely different countenance from that which emptied into the Irish Sea.

Rising majestically from this shallow trickling stream is Blease Fell, upon which stands the Heart of Westmorland. Passing Dillicar we were directly opposite this wood and, for a fleeting moment, we could appreciate the full significance of the perfectly-shaped heart; as soon as we passed, the outline faded. In the romantic myths of legend it is believed that a young Yorkshire swain walked over the fells to wed his lady-love, only to find that he had been jilted for another. Broken-hearted, he planted the woods in the shape of a heart, albeit a broken one, while the four little trees to the side are supposed to represent tear-drops. A beautiful and sad story but, no doubt, based on some sort of fact.

As we were now approaching the last set of troughs in England, I walked across to the 'dip' and released the chain. Running alongside us was a near perpendicular wall of rock, and as I concentrated on it from the speeding footplate, it suddenly curved groundwards and vanished. This was my cue to wind down the scoop, and when this operation was completed, we were running into Tebay.

The hills rising high on all sides seemed reluctant to allow the sun to penetrate this sparse dwelling place. We were now at the start of the heavy incline known as Shap, so I shovelled a terrific amount of coal into the firebox, giving the engine plenty to chew on as she made her laborious progress up the 7¾ mile climb. Sticking gamely to her task she blasted the smoke-laden exhaust high in the atmosphere, before it descended and rolled away over the barren wilderness. Even on such a lovely day as this, the landscape was bleak and hostile, devoid of all greenery except for the burnt coarse brown grass that covered the arid ground. As we neared Scot Green a couple of wild ponies abruptly stopped grazing, threw up their heads and cantered away to a more peaceful area; a place where they would not be disturbed by a roaring monster belching filthy pollution. The fact that they were wild was verified by the absence of shoes on their hooves.

From our vantage point on the footplate, we could survey several square miles of barren moorland. Over to the north-west, however, and totally out of keeping with this inhospitable region of uncultivated tract of land was an hotel, complete with tennis court. As our gaze moved a little more north-wards, another unusual object caught our eye — a statue of Queen Victoria standing in the middle of nowhere.

Passing Shap Wells, I stoked the fire for what I hoped would be the last time up this murderous incline, for we were now very near the summit. Having done this, I settled down for a smoke, one that had been well-earned. Running over the top I reflected that we were now as high as the top of the Eiffel Tower, 916ft. above sea-level. Quarries are numerous in this part of the country, and we passed several before making a brief stop at Shap, a thinly-populated area of stone houses, but little else.

At Thrimby Grange the River Leith, a mere stream, ran alongside then ducked underneath the track before we reached Bessy Ghyll. The word 'ghyll', sometimes spelt 'gill', is of Anglo-Saxon origin, and simply means a torrent. It passed the old water-mill, now defunct, then veered away through Great Strickland. Bessy Ghyll Woods, on our left, are on the very perimeter of Lowther Park, which stretches for some six miles. In this great park is Lowther Castle, of which we were offered a fleeting glimpse before we reached Eden Valley, where the line from Kirkby Stevens joined ours.

With little weight on the drawbar, due to the falling gradient, our 'Royal Scot' pitched and rolled in a deplorable fashion, so my driver was obliged to check her speed as she rounded the bend over the River Lowther, although she was steady as she passed over the Eamont into Penrith. The road from here was fairly level, past Kitchen Hill, then Plumpton, and downhill through Calthwaite to Southwaite.

Thwaite, a word of Scandinavian origin, means a piece of land converted to tillage, but is now used only in place names and is quite common in the North of England. At Southwaite there is one thoroughfare, a little public house (appropriately called the 'Station Inn') and a telephone kiosk. From here we passed the old station house of Wreay, and descended past Upperby Marshalling Yards, then over a veritable maze of points to enter Carlisle Citadel Station.

This, then, is the colourful and picturesque road to the north; bleak sometimes and perhaps hostile, but never boring and always interesting.

CHAPTER NINE

The Motor Link

A few years passed and I was promoted to the 'motor-link', which was made up of six weeks work including three late shifts, two early morning turns and one beginning at 10.15a.m. The trains we manned were local passenger workings, serving an area encompassed by perhaps a ten mile radius. The motive power was provided by 2-4-2 tank engines, fitted with vacuum-controlled regulators enabling the train to be driven from the coach, and known as motor engines. We would haul the two coach train on the outward journey, to return with the coaches leading, and the engine propelling at the rear — hence the term 'push and pull'.

When running motor first, the driver would be positioned in the leading coach with two handles under his control, one for the brake and the other manipulating the regulator on the locomotive. As this type of work entailed the fireman being alone on the footplate, he had to undergo a test by an Inspector, who examined him on rules and his ability to operate the locomotive without supervision. Within easy reach of the driver was also a bell-push, similar to those commonly seen on any front door. This was used to communicate with the fireman, and a prescribed number of rings was visibly displayed on a notice-board for each operation. A corresponding number of rings was on the footplate of every motor engine; that this did not always tally was incidental.

When the driver was ready to leave the starting point, he would signal '2 pause 2', which advised the fireman to open the regulator and start the train, and as the train gathered speed he would then notch the reversing gear to the right setting. According to regulations the fireman left the regulator open until completion of the journey, the driver using the vacuum-control to close it, then opening it again when required. Had the men worked to this routine, I'm afraid the train would have been pushed through every station, as the regulator admitted steam to the cylinders even after it had been closed in the driving compartment; therefore the firemen did the obvious, they closed it by hand. This was a gross contravention of the regulations, and woe betide the men concerned if a footplate inspector happened to board the train. I might hastily add, that this in no way jeopardised the safety of the passengers, as the driver was always in complete control.

One of our early shifts was to work the 7a.m. motor-engine to Rainford Junction. Leaving St. Helens, we called at six stations on the picturesque Rainford Branch; this was part of the Lord Stanley estate and in complete contrast to the smoky, grimy atmosphere of St. Helens and its obnoxious smells, only a short distance away. They were delightful little stations, and all had charming names. The road was double track to Rookery, but then a 'staff' had to be procured before entering the single line to Rainford Village. Leaning out of the window, the 'bobby' simply held it at arm's length, and the fireman would grab it as the engine passed. Upon leaving the village, however, the staff had to be given up and another one taken; a procedure that required a little more dexterity. The fireman would sort of wedge his legs between the small bunker and the side tank, then place his knees behind the handrails, thus leaving both hands free. The 'bobby' would hold the staff in his right hand, with the left hand lower down, the fireman corresponding in the opposite posture and holding the staff to be given up in his lower hand. Thus with the right hand held high, he would simply close his fist as soon as he felt wood touch flesh.

A short run to the junction took us into the back platform to connect our passengers with the Wigan to Southport line. Afterwards, when the travellers from the express had embarked with us, we set off to St. Helens, calling at all the halts along the way. This time, though, we would run motor first, the fireman being alone on the footplate.

We were scheduled to be relieved at Warrington at 12.59p.m. with the relief crew working the 1.01p.m. service to Rainford; simply a repetition of our morning's work. This duty followed the 7a.m. turn, and we would be working it the following week. This afternoon turn expired as we arrived at Warrington with the 7p.m. service from St. Helens, when we would put the train in the small carriage sidings. When it was safely on the stop block the fireman would disconnect the locomotive, a simple task which could sometimes develop complications. As on the morning job, the fireman would couple up by means of the shackle, tightening it to alleviate buffering of the train and the engine. When this was done and, according to regulations these were the first items to be coupled, both the brake-pipes and the regulator-pipes would be connected, and then the steam-pipes, if the train needed to be heated. After these had all been joined up, it was an easy chore to slot the jumper cables into position; this simply made electrical contact of the bell from coach to engine.

Then there was the whistle-cord to be hooked up, and to do this the fireman had to make a perilous ascent on to the bunker, this being particularly precarious if the engine was high with coal. He then had to reach towards the train, grab the cord hanging down from the coach while, at the same time, keeping his equilibrium of balance, and tie it to the piece hanging from the cab of the engine. Often this would be trapped by coal, and if it was large and lumpy it could be the devil's own work to release it.

Of course, when we were stabling the train, all this took place in reverse as it were, and the fireman, not infrequently, forgot about the whistle. He and his driver would soon be reminded of this by an earsplitting sound, which would end abruptly in the snap of the cord. Indeed, on a number of occasions, much the same thing happened when a careless fireman did not put the shackle on first and then, when all else had been coupled, he would forget it altogether. Upon receiving the 'right away', the engine would travel a few yards before coming to an unceremonious halt, with vacuum-pipes trailing along the floor and the brakes being automatically applied.

It was impossible to keep clean on local passenger services, due to the engines being small and dirty and the caking of oil on the shackles. After working in this link for about a year, I was promoted to a link which contained five weeks of 'double-trip' work out of twelve. I was not sorry to leave the motor link, and enjoyed working these trips to Carlisle. It was lucky for me that I did, for I was to remain on these jobs for seven years during which time I had a variety of mates; some good ones, some who were not so bad and an odd one or two who were downright terrible. Towards the end of my term in this link I was to 'pass out' for driving duties, thus starting another stage in my career as a passed fireman.

33 Working a freight train of open wagons and closed vans through
Oxenholme is LMS 'Jubilee' No. 5595 *Southern Rhodesia*, with the
smaller tender.

V. R. Anderson Collection

34 'Black Five' No. 44675 steams through Oxenholme with a 'mixed' train
on 25th August 1967.

V. R. Anderson

35 Ex-LMS 'Black Five', No. 44816, heads a mixed freight through Scout Green, Shap, on 21st August 1967.

V. R. Anderson

36 Shap Summit signal box, 17th August 1954.

British Rail

37 The southern approach to Carlisle (Citadel) Station, now very much changed in appearance since electrification.

British Rail

38 LMS 'Royal Scot' No. 6133 *The Green Howards*, leaves Carlisle with a 'down' Scottish express in 1947.

V. R. Anderson Collection

39 A Carlisle (Kingmoor)-allocated ex-LMS 'Jinty', No. 47471, stands in the sunshine at its home depot, and displays the 'lion on wheel' emblem on the tank side.

V. R. Anderson Collection

40 Ex-LMS 'Jinty' No. 47345 prepares to take on its next shunting duty at Carlisle (Upperby) in July 1963.

A. G. Ellis

41 Acton Grange Viaduct signal box, photographed in August 1939. This box spans the main Crewe to Warrington line, north of Winsford.

V. R. Anderson Collection

42 Ellesmere Port Station, pictured on 4th April 1972, showing clearly the ornate station building, road overbridge and the through line from West Kirby to Warrington (ex-Birkenhead Joint Railway).

V. R. Anderson

43 The derelict engine shed building at Ellesmere Port.

G. Fox

44 Ellesmere Port Station, as seen on 4th April 1972, showing also the timber-built engine shed, long since disused.

V. R. Anderson

45 A general view of Chester Station, photographed on 18th September 1956, showing the overall roof and a party of workmen awaiting their train.

British Rail

46 The approach to Chester (General) Station, showing the mass of semaphore signals that once adorned this area.

D. P. Rowlands

47 A view from ex-LNWR Saltney Ferry passenger station, showing Mold Junction Shed in the background.

Lens of Sutton

48 Mold Junction No. 1 signal box, as seen on 4th April 1972.

V. R. Anderson

49 'Royal Scot' class 4-6-0, No. 46153 *The Royal Dragoon*, waits in platform 4 at Crewe in preparation to depart with the 'up' 'Royal Scot' on 2nd June 1953, Coronation Day; hence the crown on the front of the locomotive.

V. R. Anderson Collection

50 No. 5540 *Sir Robert Turnbull*, an ex-LMS 'Patriot', prior to receiving its double chimney, prepares to leave the covered Rugby Station with an express.

J. Coltas

51 An LMS 5XP 'Jubilee', No. 5647 *Sturdee*, stands outside Rugby Shed in 1936. This class of locomotive was introduced in 1934.

J. Coltas

52 A mixed freight, headed by 'Jubilee' No. 5733 *Novelty*, passes through wooded scenery, prior to nationalisation and renumbering.

British Rail

53 Ex-LNWR 0-8-0, No. 9012, of the class referred to in the text, awaits
return to duty. This particular locomotive was designed by Webb in
1892 and was rebuilt by Whale in 1908.

V. R. Anderson Collection

54 No. 49140 is another Whale-rebuilt Webb LNWR 0-8-0, and the
smaller style British Railways number and emblem is in evidence.

British Rail

55 An LMS 'Crab', No. 2727, stands beneath the coaling plant before taking on its next duty. This particular 'Crab' is allocated to Low Moor.

V. R. Anderson Collection

56 One of the 2-8-0 'Crabs', introduced in 1926 by the LMS, No. 2887, photographed prior to nationalisation in 1948.

V. R. Anderson Collection

57 LMS-built 0-6-0 No. 4411, carrying a Bristol (22A) shed plate, one of the types of engine mentioned in the text, hauling a mixed freight.

Lens of Sutton

58 A Carlisle-allocated ex-LMS 4F 0-6-0 stands beside 'Black Five' No. 45082 during an off-duty session.

V. R. Anderson Collection

59 No. 52592, a 1909 Hughes-designed ex-L&YR 0-6-0 3F, stands beside an interesting looking water column in June 1953, at Mirfield. These locomotives bring back many memories.

V. R. Anderson Collection

60 An ex-L&YR 3F, No. 52515 of the class designed by Aspinall in 1889, showing the open cab and low tender.

V. R. Anderson Collection

61 No. 46203 *Princess Margaret Rose*, a 'Princess Royal' class Pacific locomotive, showing the British Railways 'lion on wheel' crest on the tender.

V. R. Anderson Collection

62 The Camden-based 'Patriot', No. 5550, mentioned in the text, is pictured in 1935 soon after its introduction. This locomotive was never named.

V. R. Anderson Collection

63 An ex-L&YR 0-6-0 Aspin[...]
3F locomotive, No. 12120,[...]
the same class as Nos. 121[...]
and 12102, mentioned in t[...]
text, is pictured displa[...]
ing one of the old type she[...]
plates (No. 26) indicatin[...]
allocation to Hellifield.

V. R. Anderson Collecti[...]

64 The author looks from t[...]
cab window of 1952-bu[...]
350hp diesel shunter, N[...]
12100, which was built [...]
Derby Works.

S. Cheetha[...]

CHAPTER TEN

Maiden Trip, London

It was the week before the annual leave period of 1948, and the custom was to promote eleven sets of men into a newly-created link so that they could work in the place of the men on holiday. This, coupled with the fact that two drivers had retired recently and one had died, meant that I would be advanced fourteen spaces up the ladder of promotion.

After the motor-link, the next link in order of seniority was No. 2 freight, more commonly known as the Carlisle link, which consisted of twelve weeks' work. The next one above this was No. 1 freight, known as the London link, and having a duration of eight weeks, and as there was only one job to Camden it meant doing three 'double-trips' one week, then the two trips four weeks later. On the two trips, which were on the Tuesday and Thursday, the week's work was made up by a single trip before and after.

The booking off turns in the Carlisle link were spaced out in a more haphazard manner; the night job of three trips (one week's work) and the two trips of Tuesday and Thursday were only a fortnight apart. The morning job (six turns) was spread over three weeks, and an early morning Sunday turn was pressed in between a Saturday early local job and a Tuesday afternoon shift. We would be working home for our Monday turn. These 'double-trips' were so widely spread among the twelve weeks that one of our drivers came to the conclusion that Warrington men were either going to Carlisle, were on the road back from Carlisle or were already at Carlisle taking rest, during the whole of the 168 hours from Saturday midnight to the next Saturday midnight.

As I was the senior hand in the motor-link, and was due to advance fourteen places, I found that I had skipped the Carlisle link altogether and was marked in the London link, starting on the week's work containing the two 'double-trips' to Camden. My mate was to be Billy Crankshaw, a man of slight stature for whom I had not fired previously. However, as we would be on a local trip job on the Monday, it gave both of us ample opportunity to get acquainted. He was a friendly type, a bit of a stiff shirt perhaps, but quite amiable and easy to get along with. To say he liked the London work would have been a gross understatement; he talked of little else whilst we were tripping wagons from one yard to another. During the conversation about the road to London, I could not help detecting the prime factor for his liking of the job, this being the mileage payment involved; if and when we had completed 140 miles, we were paid over and above this at the rate of one hour's pay for each additional fifteen miles beyond this distance. I might hastily add that although this was an incentive, it could possibly turn out to be no extra at all because if we worked, say, 170 miles, which would be equivalent to ten hours work, at the same time if we had a bad road it could easily take us this length of time to achieve it, meaning we would be no better off except for the overtime which we had already worked anyway.

On Tuesday evening, at 7.25p.m., I met my mate at the shed and he did not seem at all pleased. When I politely asked him why the glum face, he told me to have a look at the engine board. Where the engine number of our locomotive should have been was the word 'cape'; this word had infiltrated into our jargon and all enginemen knew what it meant, although they did not know from what source it was derived. The truth is that as a telephone boy, it had been my job to translate the coded messages I received from the telegraph office, and the word 'cape' simply meant that a certain train had been cancelled. This was the reason for Billy's lack of joy; we would now have to travel to Willesden as passengers. This was all very nice and comfortable, as I would not have to slog away feeding coal into a hungry firebox for 180 miles, but on the other hand we would not receive any mileage payment. As our train did not arrive in Euston until 4.30a.m., it would mean we would be on duty about 10½ hours by the time we had made our way back to Willesden. This I explained to my mate, but right away I could tell by his dogmatic attitude he had made up his mind that he was the victim of a cruel twist of fate, so I gave up trying to convince him; I did not want to cause any animosity.

We took rest in the barracks at Willesden and, after a fairly good sleep, we rose to a fine day that was not too hot, but was sunny, with no cloud. After a quick meal we caught a train to the great city itself, and spent a few pleasant hours in the heart of London before returning to our lodge. When we had eaten a light meal of tea and sandwiches, we collected our personal belongings, and adjourned to Willesden Shed to book on at 7.12p.m. Taking the local train to Chalk Farm (known now as Primrose Hill), we walked to the shunters' cabin to deposit our 'traps', as we called our personal gear, before retiring to the 'Pembroke Arms' to enjoy a couple of pints whilst waiting for our train to be marshalled ready for us to take to Froghall, Warrington.

The engine on the return trip was always the same one we brought from the north, but as we had not worked down the previous night we would now be allocated a Camden locomotive. When we climbed aboard my heart sank — it was a Stanier Class 5 2-6-0, a type of engine I strongly detested for a host of reasons. The main fault with them was that the fireman could not sit down and rest his arm on the handrest, as this was almost level with his knees, and the lack of height of the cab roof prevented him from putting his head out unless his shoulders were also out of the cab; truly a dangerous practice, apart from the discomfort. It was when the men had alighted from the footplate that I noticed the oil box, which acted as a seat, had no lid on it. I swung from the cab and hunted round for a piece of wood of any description, as I had no intention of standing up on the long haul home. Fortunately I soon found a piece that would suffice, and we were on our way. When I picked up the shovel I noticed the state of the tender; the coal was 'well back', and I knew it would not be long before I would be in the tender scraping the coal forward with the coal pick.

At 8.50p.m. prompt we began the stiff drag out of Camden Yard, and as I busied myself putting on a generous amount of coal round the firebox we entered the tunnel, situated immediately at the outlet of the yard. I slammed the firehole shut, as I wanted to create a rather large fire, and in order to do this, without choking it by putting too much on too quickly, I would endeavour to place a little on at rapid intervals. This would give the coal the chance to ignite and, indeed, conformed to the rule of firing 'little and often'. The whole idea of this scientific method was to expose more area of coal to naked heat. Indeed, if a big fire was put on all at once the coal underneath would be covered with more coal, and therefore would have to remain 'cold' whilst the coal above and below was being ignited. By firing frequently the coal had a chance of burning through and then igniting the next round of coal, thus making up a large well-burnt fire. Once the grate, the brick arch and the whole firebox was well and truly hot, it made the job of keeping steam up to the pressure mark that much easier.

I knew it would be no picnic humping fifty laden wagons all the way home and, indeed, the road from Camden climbed steadily all the way to Tring, some thirty miles to the north.

By Willesden we had gathered some speed, but the locomotive was working at full capacity and would not increase her rate of progress now until we topped Tring Cutting. I had to nurse her like a baby, giving her more coal but being very careful not to over-fire her. I also had to keep the boiler well up the glass because once the water level dropped, the pressure would be jeopardised and then it would take a tremendous amount of skill and ingenuity to bring the boiler back to normal. The piece of wood I had procured for a makeshift seat had hardly been used, but Froghall was a long way off and I would be glad of it long before we arrived home.

As we passed Tring the engine began to accelerate briskly, and Billy notched the wheel back. When this was done we were pestered by the knock of the big ends, due to the small driving wheels and the fact that when the wheel was notched up, expansion and compression was taking place at the same time in the same cylinder, although on opposite sides of the piston. The fire was now burning well with a yellowish white glow, and after spreading another charge of coal round the box I indulged in a well-earned sit down. The tender of this class was less than the width of the footplate by some 2ft., thus rendering no protection at all to the driver on one side and the fireman, if he was sitting down, on the other. Due to the lack of height of the tender, a yawning gap was open to the elements right beneath the cab roof.

Approaching Leighton Buzzard on the slow line, I waited until we had passed the station, and then I rammed the blower on hard, for we were about to enter a nasty little tunnel. From the top of the chimney to the roof of the tunnel was a mere couple of inches, and the sides of the cab were just as close to the walls of the tunnel. With the blower on as hard as it would go, and the firehole door shut tightly, I leaned forward as far as I possibly could with my handkerchief round my mouth, my driver doing likewise. Even this did not prevent a terrific back-flash from the firehole as we hit the entrance of that 'hole in the wall'. We were quickly through but happy to be out in the fresh air again, because although it was short it was a nasty piece of work.

We stormed through Bletchley and were soon on the way to Roade, a junction where we could be turned either through Northampton, on the

road which veered away to the right, or carry on along the straight road to
Blisworth and Kilsby tunnels before running down into Rugby. We were
kept to the main line, and arrived at Rugby on time. Here we were scheduled to be examined by the carriage & wagon staff, and for this we were
allowed 26 minutes.

Coming to a stand, with our tank filling hole opposite the water-column, I
shouted 'Whoa' to my mate then clambered up the tender to fill the tank.
This took precious time, as by now we were hungry and ready for something
to eat, so as soon as the tank was full I skipped back on to the footplate and
hastily consumed a sandwich. The respite did not last long, however, and in
no time at all we were pulling out of Rugby on the final lap of the 100 miles
to Warrington. Somehow, once on the right side of Rugby, it seemed for the
first time that we were really on the way home. This was another peculiar
aspect of these jobs; that the road back never seemed as far as the road
going down.

Brinklow was passed in fine style, and Nuneaton flashed by dead on
schedule. Negotiating the twisting line at Atherstone, then flying past
Polesworth, we headed for Tamworth with the distant signals all in our
favour. I then stoked the engine in readiness for the trough because soon I
was to pick up water; a tricky affair to say the least. After passing through
Tamworth the next box was Coton Crossing, followed by Hademore Crossing, with the troughs being situated between the two. Now, as the names
imply, the 'crossings' were literally places for road traffic to cross the railroad. My 'landmark' for the commencement of these troughs was a certain
number of telegraph poles from the distant signal, and in order to count
these correctly I had to bend down, so I could see the skyline, then count
seven poles and lower the scoop. Alas, there was no indication when we
were over them, and if the scoop was left in a second or two longer than it
should be it would be knocked off by the wooden sleepers raised to rail level
at the point of road access. Somehow, we took it all in our stride, and rarely
did we have any trouble from lost scoops.

Thus with a full tank we passed through Lichfield and away past
Armitage, on towards Colwich, through Shugborough Tunnel, Queensville
and then on to the left-hand curve before swinging right-handed through
Stafford. From here the road climbed steeply for about ten miles then, at
the summit of this incline, Madeley Troughs. After topping the tank to
capacity I sat down to enjoy a smoke, with an easy descent for the next ten
miles to Crewe. Here we were turned through the sidings, as few goods
trains were allowed through the station. Even so, it was classed as a main
line, therefore it did not take long to negotiate the few boxes. Soon we were
being let out on to the main line proper, at Coalyard, and then it was plain
sailing for the last twenty miles to Warrington where we left the main line,
to steam gently up the slow line to Froghall. The time was 2.12a.m. and I
was not sorry to arrive, so I hooked the engine from the train and proceeded
to Dallam Shed, to berth the locomotive and complete my maiden voyage to
London.

CHAPTER ELEVEN

London and Carlisle

It was now Thursday morning, and we would be booking on that same evening. The job was simply a matter of bed and work, although we did earn a trifle more money on 'double-trips' and, of course, this made it all worthwhile; after all we were here to make a living, so we made the best of it.

We arrived at 7.25p.m. that evening to find our locomotive was No. 5095, a Warrington engine, and as we knew our own locomotives this was not a bad one. We prepared her for the road and then adjourned to 'Annie's', the little local inn, where we enjoyed a couple of pints before setting off on the long road to Willesden. Without this deviation from the straight and narrow, as it were, the job would have been tedious and boring.

Hooking on to our train at Arpley, subsequently obtaining the required amount of vacuum and receiving the details of our load from the guard, we set forth on the first stage of the 183 mile trip, with Rugby as our first stop. Here, as on the return trip, we were marked to be examined by C&W men, and then, if everything was in order, proceed on the last lap to London. The trip went well and, apart from the routine job of stoking the engine and keeping the boiler up to the mark, nothing out of the ordinary happened, and we arrived at Willesden to be relieved at 2.10a.m.

Going through the usual procedure of having a light meal, a wash, and then retiring to bed in the barracks at Willesden, we eventually rose and, after another light refreshment, made our way into the city. We spent a pleasant day at Kew Gardens, having a snack and a couple of beverages before catching a train back to our billet. Before we left the 'barracks' we had a substantial meal, which would sustain us on our way home. We took the train to Chalk Farm, dumped our cases in the cabin, then made our way to 'The Pembroke'. We sat there enjoying the quiet tranquility, and relaxing whilst not many people were in the hotel, when all at once, the whole pub was plunged into darkness. Not knowing what had happened we sat there until the lights were put back on but, horror of horrors, our feet were ankle deep in water. During the brief time we had been in the bar a cloudburst had occurred, flooding the place out and also fusing the lights. We left with wet shoes and socks. After a more or less routine trip we arrived home, though not overjoyed by the prospect of booking on on Saturday night.

Our last duty of the week was to work a train to Crewe, turn the engine, then plod back in the early hours of Sunday morning. This signalled the end of a rather hard week's graft and, apart from the fact that we had earned a little extra in the way of mileage payment, and something extra for night rate, we were quite relieved to have the week behind us.

The following Monday, which came all too quickly, saw us on a 'decent' day turn, namely the 8.30a.m. service to Middlewich. The locomotive was prepared for us by another set of men, and we were due off the shed at 8.05a.m. Leaving South End Yard with a heavy mineral train, we plodded up Acton Grange before gathering a bit of speed down through Moore and on to Acton Bridge, where we switched to the slow line for Hartford and then on to the Northwich branch. We then dropped down a slight incline, through some of the most picturesque landscape of the County of Cheshire, and into Northwich. After detaching the engine we proceeded on to the shed, where we turned her round, came off again and backed up for Middlewich. From Northwich we procured a 'staff', as the line was signalled under the single line regulations. Although it was not far to our destination the line passed through beautiful scenery with herons, coots, moorhens and a host of other wild creatures inhabiting this lovely countryside. It was thoroughly enjoyable, and we arrived all too soon at Middlewich to begin shunting, after we had given up the staff to the signalman at this outlandish little box. Upon finishing our work we then had to run tender first back to Northwich where, once again, we had to shunt our train so that the engine was at the front and the brake van in the rear. From here it was plain sailing, as we only had to work back to Warrington and place our train in the private sidings of J. Crosfield & Sons.

It probably does not seem much of a day's work, but it took us the best part of ten hours to complete this diagram. Although the time on duty was desirable, the job was such that we barely had time to eat our midday snack; we were on the go the whole day, finishing when the engine was safely berthed on the shed, which was usually about 5.30p.m.

Until recently our working week had consisted of 48 hours but now, happily, this had been cut to 44. In order to implement this and, at the same time keep to our eight hour day, we were set to work six turns one week then five the following week, thus giving an 88 hour fortnight of eleven eight hour shifts. The Local Departmental Committee (the three men appointed to foster our welfare) thought that by having the five day weeks on the day turns, and the six day weeks on the late shifts, they would create more day work. I'm afraid they were under an illusion, because if the late turns had been given a day off, a man may have been able to attend a function specified by a date, which would not be available to him later when on a more suitable turn. It would also have split the week in two, and would have made a late shift a little more palatable. As it was, the simple fact remained that we still had to work the same shifts, no matter how they were spread round the links. Still, it was quite pleasant to have a lazy day at least once when on early turn. The day, aptly called a 'rest day', was staggered over the link, as far as possible, to give an equal number of Saturdays in each of the links.

Two weeks after working the two trips to London we were given an afternoon job to Bamfurlong, not a great way from our home depot. We were something of a travelling shunting engine, picking up and putting off at various points along the route. Although a trifle boring, the job was quite a comfortable task, and we usually finished in under eight hours. A fortnight later and we would be on the three trips to Camden, covering more than a thousand miles for our week's work. Starting on Monday night we knew we would be 'in harness' until early Sunday morning; a gruelling week without doubt. If the weather was bad with, for example, rain, fog or falling snow, it would be that much more hazardous. When the weather was kind, though, the job presented a glorious opportunity to see the greatest city in the world, and I was thankful for the years I spent firing to London. Like all other firemen I had my share of rough trips, but they were forgotten in the pleasure I derived from the excursions I made round the city.

I found that the most important factor when 'double-trip' firing was to have a good mate. Fortunately we did not remain too long with one driver, whether good or bad, because when holidays ended at the end of September it was time for the 'grand put back', when we would, more or less, be back where we were before the holidays started. In my case I went back eleven spaces, and this resulted in my being in the Carlisle link for the whole of the winter. Thus in the autumn of that year, I was marked with yet another driver, and I knew that, all being well, we would be together for the next eight months or so until the start of the following year's annual leave period.

My mate was a rather unusual person. An ex-Navy man, he had earned himself the nickname of 'Sailor', and the first feature I noticed was his cleanness, a slightly different meaning to the word 'cleanliness'. His canvas-topped 'chinny' was always polished to a fine shine, while his russet face looked equally polished, with never a sign of a whisker. His overalls were always spotlessly clean, and his shoes were well brushed with a deep shine. He was a good engineman who never flogged the engine unnecessarily, and we were friends right from the start. One of his practices when on 'double-trips' was to bring two pies, often steak and kidney, and these he would put on the screenplate as we left the Warrington area. By the time we were up in the mountains, probably somewhere around Grayrigg, these would give off a wonderful aroma as they began to warm. Old Sailor would then take out his knife and cut one in half, offering me a whole one. One can easily imagine how I felt after firing an engine all this way, working up an appetite and being tempted ravishingly by the scrumptious smell coming from the screenplate. Needless to say it did not take me long to do justice to the pie, but then, my mate, who had eaten only half of one, would look at me, smile, then say something about me being young and having a healthy appetite. Almost without fail I would be given the other half of his, thus having three times more than he had.

It so happened that the guards we had on this run had the same number of weeks in their link, so it was the guard that was on this job at the outset who would be with us on each subsequent trip throughout the winter. The guard we had on the 8.30p.m. working from Froghall was an eccentric person who was always referred to as 'Mad Mac'; a nickname he used even when referring to himself. To say he knew the rule book would have been a tremendous understatement; he knew it like he knew 'Mary had a Little Lamb'. It was this knowledge of rules, which he asserted at all times (woe betide the unfortunate victim who dared contradict him), that had earned him his dubious *nom de plume*.

It does not leave much to the imagination, then, to visualise just what I was teamed up with. These were the two men I was to work with, and also lodge with for what was most of the week when on the three 'double-trips' to

Carlisle. When booked off, the time spent in the hostel was anything up to sixteen hours, a long time to be at leisure, if this could be called leisure, and where most other drivers and guards would make an excursion into the town, these two characters, with whom I was destined to work as a team, had other ideas. Each would arise, after he had had his sleep, and take off on some unknown excursion, alone. What is perhaps more strange, they never disclosed the whereabouts of their solitary meanderings.

All in all, though, the winter months spent firing to Carlisle were quite pleasant, and the social atmosphere on the footplate left nothing to be desired. When the holiday period loomed on the working horizon once more, it was with a feeling of reluctance, tempered with a sense of sadness, that we awaited the new working sheets, which would tell us to which fresh mates we were assigned. I was once again marked in the London link, this time with a driver by the name of Norman Brown, while 'Sailor' was teamed with a fireman whom he clearly did not like. The first week of the new schedules saw 'Sailor' on the three trips to Carlisle, and he asked me to exchange turns with the fireman with whom he had just been freshly marked. I said I was not too keen on the idea, but he persisted and, finally, I agreed.

'Oh good,' he said, 'I'll buy you twenty Capstan for exchanging him'. I told him he need not, that I was just doing him a favour, so he left it at that.

The cigarettes were forgotten but, true to his word, when we were starting for home on Saturday afternoon on the third return trip, old 'Sailor' handed me a packet of cigarettes. I thanked him, and then looked at what he had given me. They were certainly not Capstan and indeed, they were a brand I had never even heard of; they were called 'Sport', a name I have never encountered since. I smiled to myself, and wondered how on earth he had come to possess this unique packet of unknown cigarettes. That was typical of 'Sailor', keeping his word as far as not breaking his promise yet procuring something that could not have been obtained by the straight-forward action of convention.

Upon finishing at Dallam we parted and I wished him luck, knowing he would not be quite so happy with his present fireman. He thanked me for all I had done to make the job pleasant, and went on his way. A few weeks later I heard he had applied to come off the Carlisle run, and had opted for shunt-ing engine duties. As for me, I took up duties in the London link again and started on the Middlewich job. Norman and I seemed to fit together right from the start; he liked a flutter on the horses, and so did I. He also loved a pint which, of course, I did too. He was a veteran of World War I and many times, whilst awaiting signals, he would tell me of his exploits in the Army, and the humorous descriptions of his adventures made interesting listen-ing. The following week saw us working the two trips, on Tuesday and Thursday to Willesden and, as was usual, we adjourned to 'Annie's' after we had prepared the engine. He was a wonderful companion when off duty, and to say he knew his way round London would have been putting it mildly; he knew every inch, or so it appeared.

Our next job, a week later, was the Winwick Quay to Birkenhead run, a straightforward duty starting at 6.10a.m. which involved going light to the Quay, working to Birkenhead and then going home 'on the cushions'. But this particular morning, after we had prepared the locomotive, the Running

Foreman told us to take another engine of the same class. Of course, by this time, our personal belongings had been stowed on the 'Super D' we had made ready and then, as we were transhipping all the tools from one engine to the other, we were quite busy and eager to leave the depot; the quicker we did the job the sooner we would be at home.

All went well until we arrived at Daresbury; here we were ordered to back inside, whilst a more important train passed. This was not unusual, and I had pleasant thoughts of having my breakfast while standing out of the way. As soon as we cleared the signal controlling the outlet on to the main line, my mate gave a 'pop' on the whistle to indicate we were clear, so I dropped the dampers and put the injector to work to keep the engine quiet or, in other words, so she would not blow off. Then I settled down to partake of my sandwiches. I had eaten nothing before turning out to work, for the simple reason that I had stayed in bed until the last possible minute, thus jeopardising my morning snack. It was when I put my hand into the coat box, where we also kept our food on this class of locomotive, that I received a nasty shock. With slow descending horror it dawned on me, like a shower of cold water, that my coat and sandwiches were still on that other engine at Dallam Shed. It wasn't that I was hungry; I was absolutely famished. Without more ado I sped off to the signal box, where I phoned the time-keeper at Dallam to explain the unfortunate plight into which I had landed myself. He said he would go and retrieve them and I thanked him, but that did not solve the problem of my unappeased hunger. My mate laughed about it, not maliciously, but nevertheless it made me mad and I told him he should not laugh at other people's downfalls. There was one bright spot, my mate informed me I had not forgotten the brew can.

Eventually we set off again and, in due course, pulled into Ellesmere Port to put traffic off and pick up wagons destined for Hooton and Birkenhead. We had to run right over the points, almost to the station, so I dropped from the footplate, with can in hand, and headed for a little hut which was designed to serve as a canteen for the local workforce. It bore the solitary name of 'Sylvia's'; well, I thought, I hope Sylvia can rescue me from the pangs of hunger. Tantalisingly on display were some lovely barm cakes, deliciously made up with boiled ham and mouth watering salad. A quick calculation prompted me to ask for six of them; four for me, I reckoned, and two for Norman. With these and a can of freshly-brewed tea, I set off to where my mate was busily shunting some three or four hundred yards away. Close to the side of the track were some sleepers, neatly piled ready for plate-layers to replace. They looked inviting, so I sat on them and tucked into the tea and the bag of goodies. They were marvellous, and the first one vanished in a trice. Then the next, and another. Gosh! There were only two left, yet the temptation was too great and I succumbed; there were none left.

I swung aboard the footplate and, as my mate drew level, I rather sheepishly explained what I had done. It was Norman's turn to be vexed, and the names he called me are not for repetition. It was all banter, though, and he saw the funny side of it, as I told him he could have a drink of fresh tea. Luckily for me it was not raining, as I had to make my way as a passenger from Birkenhead without a coat, which I collected upon arriving back at our home depot.

A few weeks later, a similar sort of incident happened while we were working the 11.30p.m. service to Birmingham. We worked as far as Crewe, then were relieved by Birmingham men who worked the train to their home town. The relief climbed aboard and, as they were taking off their coats, Norman started to look for his haversack. Could he find it? Not on your life! Soon the four of us were hunting round that footplate, but the haversack eluded our efforts. Norman and I reluctantly made our way to Crewe South where, fortunately, a snack could be obtained from the canteen there.

Two nights later we had the same engine, and as we were running along the road Norman stood up to adjust his seat and, lo and behold, there was the phantom haversack. It had become lodged behind the injector regulating handle, and had defied four pairs of eagle eyes to spot it. What is perhaps more remarkable, though, is how the locomotive went to Birmingham, did its work all day at that depot, worked all the way back to Warrington and still had not yielded the haversack to the men who had occupied her. It was truly amazing, but nevertheless absolutely true. Therefore Norman retrieved his bag, complete with brew can and rock hard sandwiches.

CHAPTER TWELVE

Hedging our Bets

Once again we were on the three trips, and on the first night after we had prepared the engine we adjourned to 'Annie's'. Everything was in shipshape order when we left our locomotive, so we could stay until it was almost time to ring off the shed. We eventually rang off, and proceeded to Arpley.

I knew the tank was full because I had checked the gauge but, as we approached Moore Troughs, and I crossed the footplate in readiness to lower the scoop, I noticed the gauge reading; it was at rock bottom. I brought Norman's attention to it but he shrugged, and said we would know the tank was full when we flooded it over the troughs. I dipped and left the dip in as long as I dared but it did not overflow; what is more, the gauge was still on the bottom. Was it out of order, we wondered? We had no way of telling but Norman, cool as a cucumber, said we would perhaps flood it at Whitmore.

Whitmore was passed, and with the dip in all the way along the full extent of the troughs the tank still did not overflow. Ah well, we would try again at Hademore, but the same thing occurred here also. Had we been stopped by signals I could have climbed up the tank, and looked to see how much water we had, but we were kept on the move and we did not know how much we had. On the approach to Rugby we traversed Newbold Troughs, and before we reached the end of them the tank flooded. I could not help but admire the coolness of my mate. Water was the most important commodity on a locomotive because without it, we would not get anywhere, yet Norman had proceeded along knowing full well that if that tank gauge had been reading correctly, we would have soon been in dire straits.

The week progressed and on Friday night, while having our usual couple of pints in 'Annie's', Norman handed me a sheet of paper with the names of a number of horses entered on it. They were the runners in the second race at Haydock Park the following day, so I scanned it and then asked him what was the point.

'What's going to win that race, tomorrow?' he asked.

'Oh!' I said, 'there's only one in it'.

'And what might that be?' asked Norman, frivolously.

Fiery Torch, it will walk the race', I retorted.

At this Norman burst out laughing, quite heartily.

'By Jove, I hope you are right!' he chuckled.

I was becoming annoyed, and told him to explain the mystery. This he did, telling us that he had drawn this horse in a sweep, and if it won as I had predicted then he would win £65; a princely sum by any standards. I wished him luck, and asked him if he had bet it independently — yes, he had put 5s.

on it, but when I offered to have half-a-crown with him on the bet he declined, and turned me down flatly.

'No,' he said, 'you shall not break my luck, but if it wins I will treat you!'

Away we went on the last trip of the week and the incident was forgotten, temporarily at least. When we rose at noon, I asked my mate what he had in mind for today's escapade. Still with an air of mystery about him he bade me follow him, and I found we were on a train bound for Wood Green. It was obvious he did not know his way there but, after being directed by a policeman, we were soon on the way to Alexander Park Racecourse. We walked down the path as the policeman had instructed us, but eventually the pathway ended and still we had not seen the racetrack. We walked back, and after a thorough look round we found it. I looked and saw, but did not believe my eyes, it was inconceivable that this unattractive tract of uncultivated land contained a racetrack. There were garden sheds here, haphazardly erected on unkempt allotments, and there were no proper railings, just natural barriers of freely growing hedges. Beyond this man-made jungle, somewhere in the near distance, was a little green ribbon of turf; this, then, was Ally Pally. Gosh! I had seen some nondescript dog tracks that looked more elaborate. Still, we could enjoy the thrill of the races.

I had written down four horses and told Norman that, come what may, I was not going to deviate from these; I was going to bet these and nothing else. Famous last words, as the road to hell is paved with good intentions. But I was not reckoning for the inevitable character one meets on a racetrack; the knowledgeable personality who has a friend in the know, and whose sister's Aunt Mabel does the washing for this trainer's cousin Mary, and so on. We met him, at least Norman did, for he was talking to him when I came from the bookie's, after placing a bet on the first of my four horses.

Norman seemed intently serious about the tip he had been given, a horse by the name of *Cantaquisine* that was running in the following race.

'Are you having anything on it?' asked Norman.

'I've told you, I'm only betting these on my paper'.

'Aye! OK, but he did seem genuine'.

The horse I bet in the first race won at odds of two to one, which meant I was 10s. up on my original fortune of £1. Before the next race, though, my mate had talked both himself and me to put a pound each on *Cantaquisine*.

It was an exciting race to watch, and we both had our eyes peeled for the one we had backed. It ran a fine race and, as it passed us, I shouted to Norman that it was going to win. The winning post was a little to our right as we looked at the track but, tantalisingly, in between us and the finish, was a tree which moved in the slight breeze. For the last few strides the horses were lost to view, but I was confident *Cantaquisine* was leading as they shot from sight behind that infernal tree. There was nothing for it but to wait for the official outcome, but it was maddening to see the result. Our horse had been beaten by a neck, and as we had obtained odds of eight to one, it would have been a really good bet had it matured. However, it was only marginally beaten, so we had a good run for our money. It certainly seemed that Lady Luck had turned fickle on me because, at the end of the meeting, I was, in Cockney jargon, 'borasic lint'. I had deviated from the races in which my selections ran, being impatient to wait for them to run. In fact, two were running at Haydock, but it was easy to secure a wager here even though they were running elsewhere.

How did my selections fare? No, they did not all win, but three of them did and one of them, a horse called *Trewillis*, won at the super-generous odds of twenty to one. *Wainwright*, another of my fancies, won at four to one while the third, running in the last race at 'Ally Pally', won at five to four favourite, ridden by a little-known apprentice by the name of Lester Piggott. Alas, my fortune had evaporated by this time, so it ran unbacked by me. Walking from the drab, uncolourful track, Norman bought a newspaper and, after perusing the sports section for a few brief seconds, invited me to shake hands. I asked him what the hell he was playing at, for I was not in the best of moods, due to the fact that the horses I had bet had lost, and the ones that I hadn't had won.

'It's won,' he almosted shouted, 'it's won, *Fiery Torch*, it's won!'

Oh. gosh, I had clean forgotten about this. I was happy for Norman's sake, of course.

'I'm glad it's won,' I said, 'what price is it?'

Norman told me to look for myself as he handed me the paper. I was astounded. Oh. it had won all right; it had won in a canter, pulling up by ten lengths, at the absolutely prohibitive odds of twenty to one on. My mate had won 3d. for his 5s. bet, and had I been allowed to go shares with him, I would have won the princely sum of 1½d. Neverthless, Norman had won £65 on his virtual 'cert'. Therefore the day ended on a happy note after all, and we celebrated his windfall in Piccadilly, before returning to Willesden to start our laborious journey home for the third and last time that week.

CHAPTER THIRTEEN

Passed Fireman

The rest of the summer was spent firing for Norman Brown, and when the holidays finished, at the end of September, I was once again put back into the Carlisle link. The year was 1953; Hilary had conquered Everest, Gordon Richards had won his one and only Derby on *Pinza* and our gracious Queen Elizabeth II had been crowned. An eventful year for sure and so it was for me, being a milestone in my footplate career.

Firemen were passed to become drivers in order of seniority, so a man was aware of just how many had to pass the Inspector before his turn became due, to face the difficult task ahead of him. It was the usual practice to take six at a time and, as I was included in this half dozen, I had to prepare myself. The six men designated to take the examination were called as and when their turn of duty was most convenient, therefore I did not know whether I was to be first or last of this particular group. This did not bother me unduly (one had to be clued up anyway), except that the first man to go always had some knowledgeable fact to pass on to the remainder, such as a favourite question which all Inspectors had.

Of the six in my group, I happened to be third, and I learned from the two who had already been in, that this particular Inspector was as keen as mustard on the locomotive itself; its characteristics, faults and remedies, and generally how the machine functioned. I had studied for months beforehand, a very concentrated study which, together with my own practical experience would, I hoped, be good enough to pull me through. Therefore it was no surprise when I received an official letter detailing me to be at Edge Hill on Monday morning at 9a.m. to meet Mr Johnstone, Inspector. Although it was no surprise, I must admit my heart beat a little faster as I read that note which was, to say the least, brief, blunt and to the point.

I booked on at 7.35a.m. on Monday morning to travel on the 8.15a.m. stopping train to Edge Hill, arriving at 8.55a.m. and promptly, at 9a.m. I was knocking on the door of Mr Johnson's office, to be admitted by the gentleman himself. We were the only occupants of that dreary little cubicle, for that was all it was.

'Good morning, Mr Johnson.'

'So you are Fireman Birch of Warrington. Sit down; you may smoke if you wish.'

This was it, I thought apprehensively, my test had begun. I sat down, and from a long way off, it seemed, I heard Mr Johnson's voice. He was addressing me, quite obviously, seeing there was no one else in the room.

'You are working a goods train', I heard the voice say, 'and it becomes divided. The front portion is far in advance of the rear half, which has come

to rest. I want you to tell me in your own words exactly what you would do.'
Blimey! I thought, what a question to open an examination.

I did not hesitate. I explained that I would send my fireman back to the
guard, after he had made sure that the train could be coupled again. He
would then obtain a white 'wrong line' order form from him, return to me (as
the driver) and then, and only then, I would set back on to the rear portion,
couple up and proceed normally. I then had to explain just what the white
order form was in aid of. This form, issued by the guard, authorised me to
set back in a wrong direction and also that the guard would not move his
part of the train once he had issued and signed the order. How on earth a
man could move a disabled train with no power at his disposal is something
of a mystery, but that is the rule, and that is precisely what I told the
Inspector. He accepted my answer, and went on to ask what I would do if
the drawbar had been stretched and could not be coupled. This, of course,
would entail the use of a different 'wrong line' order, guard to signalman,
and pink in colour. I would have to run forward with the vehicles I was
attached to, put them off in a convenient siding, then return, after I had seen
the order had been duly signed by the signalman along the line in the wrong
direction. There were two more 'wrong line' orders, a yellow one and a
green one, upon which I had to elaborate.

The next question was about how a C&W man would test a vacuum failure
on a train about to depart. This, then, was how the test was to be conducted, with no set pattern. I told him that the examiner would have two
discs, which he would attach to the rear vacuum-pipes. and he went on to
ask what colours they were. I did not know, as I had never seen the discs we
were discussing. Like a lot of things, they were more or less in theory, and
were never put to practical use. As I pondered on how to answer this
question, my eyes spotted the very disks on a desk in the corner, one red the
other grey. He smiled as I told him correctly, and said that not many knew
that. I smiled too, although not openly; I had guessed right.

Questions, answers and more questions, until, some three hours later, my
head was swimming; I was getting tired of taxing my brain so much. The
Inspector seemed to sense this because, pulling out his watch, he asked me
what time I had booked on duty, and then came to the conclusion that as I
had eaten my breakfast at about 7.30a.m., it was time to have lunch. I
wholeheartedly agreed. He told me to go into the waiting-room and have my
sandwiches, and to be back in an hour. I was feeling hungry but, most of all,
I needed a rest from those incessant questions.

One hour later and I was back in his office, the inner man appeased and
my mind somewhat relaxed. During the course of the afternoon, when we
were on the subject of the locomotive, I was asked as to how, when the
engine was reversed in a certain position of the wheel, the valve on one side
was moved from right forward to right back, yet the valve on the other side
did not move at all. I answered him correctly, telling him that the valve
rod imparted no movement to the valve, because it was in the very centre
of the quadrant link as the piston was at the end of its stroke. He positively beamed; there was no doubt that he loved the locomotive, and anyone
answering a difficult question like the one I had just answered must have a
great affinity both with the locomotive and his own love of the machine.
After this he seemed to cut the examination short and, just before 4p.m., he

said I could go, and to meet him the following morning at Warrington at about 8a.m. I was also to sort out from the signalman a suitable train for me to work to Crewe.

The worst part of the test was behind me, as the next part, the actual driving of a train, would present no difficulty to an 'old hand fireman'. The driving test proved to be no hardship, even though the fireman on the train I drove was some ten years older than I, but he did his job magnificently and helped me where and when I needed it. I thanked him as we alighted at Crewe, then walked to the North End to pick up another train to work back to Liverpool. There was no trouble of any kind on this trip, and then my last part of the test was to work a passenger train out of Liverpool (Lime Street). This was a stopping train, calling at all stations between Liverpool and Manchester.

The fireman on this trip was a young man, far different from the one I had on the goods working to Crewe. He thought it very funny making faces behind the back of the Inspector, little realising that he could be seen through the window which acted as a sort of mirror. The Inspector told me to take no notice of this 'fly guy', although I was in the embarrassing situation of knowing that the Inspector knew what was going on and was aware that I knew, which made it worse. I was glad, in more ways than one, when he shook my hand at Manchester, and told me I had done very well in the test and that I had passed with flying colours. I thanked him in return and caught the next train home, thankful that I had passed and relieved that now it was all behind me — I was now a passed fireman.

CHAPTER FOURTEEN

My First Driving Turn

The position of passed fireman does not actually exist; he is, in all respects, a fireman performing firing duties who is available for driving if and when the Management is in need of a driver. He could then be utilised for the higher grade duties and would be paid at a higher rate for the turn performed, provided he did at least two hour's actual driving. This, in fact, could be more of a nuisance than an asset, as he could be taken from his own job which may have involved a couple of hours' overtime. Although he would be paid more for driving (1s. per turn to be precise), he would lose on the transaction; a paradoxical situation indeed. He would also be credited with a driving turn, which would count towards the 287 turns needed to qualify for the next rate of pay, for driving duties, of course.

I performed my first driving turn about three months after being passed out. Two years later I had reached the fantastic total of six driving turns and, dwelling a little on a mathematical calculation, I came to the astonishing realisation that I would be, at this rate of progress, bordering on 130 years of age by the time I had succeeded in achieving my first year's turns (287), in order to qualify for my next rate of pay.

It was a Saturday night, and I was prepared to go to work at 10.10p.m. ready for firing to Crewe when, in answer to the call boy at my front door, I learned I was to book on earlier for extension shunt ... my first driving job. I knew that the people in charge must undoubtedly be hard-pressed for men (Saturday night not being the best time to persuade men to come to work anyway), but I was, nevertheless, thrilled.

As I walked along Winwick Road, which led to the town centre, there was a steady stream of revellers hell-bent in the direction of their Saturday night's entertainment. Yet I was not in the least bit envious of this happy throng of people because, for the first time, I was going to work as a driver! True, it was only a shunting engine that I was going to work on, but that did not rob me of the pride I felt in the fact that, tonight, I would be the captain of the ship, and master in charge.

The fireman was an old schoolmate of mine; indeed, he had been only a couple of classes below me at school, being only two years my junior. He had started on British Railways, as it had been called since 1948 when the railways had been nationalised, in his middle twenties — hence the fact that he was so far behind me in seniority. We completed our job quite comfortably and, in fact, made an hour's overtime into the bargain; the end of a good night's work.

My second turn came some months later, when I was to work a train from Llandudno as far as Edgeley where we were ourselves relieved for Leeds.

Upon climbing aboard at Arpley, I took a quick glance at the fire, knowing that the train had been on the road for some considerable time. My fireman on this trip was an 'old hand', who had the reputation of not being too energetic. When I constructively suggested that he should run the dart along the firebars to dislodge the clinker he lazily declined the action, and muttered that it would do us. When the relief climbed on at Edgeley, the driver made it clear to me that the fire should have received some attention before now, and I was on the receiving end of his wrath due entirely to my mate's laziness.

This was the penalty one had to pay for being a young driver, as the older firemen thought they could get away with almost anything, and generally omitted the respect reserved for older and more mature drivers. Indeed, there was a grim lesson to be learned here, and I made up my mind there and then that in order to gain respect one had to earn it, and it would not be gained if a person of authority let subordinates ride roughshod over him. By the same token he had to be careful not to be too overbearing otherwise his reputation as a mate would soon become suspect. I found I could assert myself in such a manner as not to be domineering, yet mean what I said.

The Running Shift Foreman had the unthankful job of deciding who was senior hand when the matter of a driving turn was in the pipeline, and when a passed fireman was going to be temporarily promoted to the rank of driver, and woe betide him if he utilised someone junior to the man whose job it should have been. There was, of course, a machinery of protest laid down by the unions if this situation occurred, in that the offended party could put in a claim for a driving turn to be credited to him. This practice was rarely operated, because the foreman involved would then receive a rocketing from the boss; the latter frowned upon the idea of two men getting a turn each for only one job performed. The foreman would similarly want to even up the score with the man who had dared bring him into disrepute with the boss. Therefore the usual outcome of such a misdemeanour would be a slanging match between the RSF and the injured victim, often pacified peacefully with a promise to 'see him right' in the immediate future.

As a young passed fireman, who was a bit 'green' to the routine habits of this precarious grade, I once put in a claim for a turn to which I was legally entitled, but the foreman responsible never spoke to me civilly again and indeed, retired still unforgiving. This, then, was the very tricky path over which the passed fireman trod; a truly unhappy role to be sure.

CHAPTER FIFTEEN

Carnforth and a Hot Box

I had not long been married, and my wife of a few months found it extremely difficult to understand what turn I would be working the following week. I could not tell her, with any degree of certainty, what time I would be going on duty the following day, due to the fact that although I was marked on a regular time as a fireman, I did not know or have any idea if and when I should be called on earlier to go driving. Sometimes it could cause domestic friction if, after I had told her I was on at such and such a time, the call boy would rap at the door, especially if it was in the early hours of the morning when no food had been packed. Later, of course, she lost interest and just turned over when I was roused from mid-morning slumbers to go to work at some ungodly hour.

There is one time in particular that I recall; it was the weekend, and my turn of duty was at 11.45a.m. At about 3a.m. in the morning the call boy rapped at the door and, upon opening the window, I was informed that I was to book on at once for a special. Now my wife, having been advised that I was not on until lunchtime, had not prepared my sandwiches because, in those days, we did not possess a fridge, and any food stored over the weekend would certainly have gone stale. I told the call boy to inform the foreman on duty that I would not be coming, as I had no food in the house. He went on his way and I climbed back into bed, but my wife had awakened with the commotion taking place and had heard everything. The names she called me were anything but complimentary, saying how I had shown her up by saying we had no food in the house. What would the men at the shed think?

'Oh! take no notice', I retorted, 'I don't get food in on the expectation of being knocked earlier, I'm not worried'.

She was not satisfied, of course, but at that time in the morning I was in no mood to argue and went back to sleep.

Three days later, as I was talking in the drivers' lobby, a young fireman was eating a meat pie, and obviously enjoying it, when the RSF came into the lobby. Upon seeing young Tommy Pratt heartily devouring the pie, he asked him who his mate was.

'Oh!' said the foreman, when Tommy told him his mate was someone else other than myself, 'I was going to tell you to save some if your mate had been Mr Birch, as he wouldn't have any to give you afterwards because he has no food'.

I smiled to myself, as the joke went completely over the heads of everyone there, except mine, of course. It was subtle, indeed, and very cleverly put. It was also obvious that my refusing to come and book on duty early

Monday morning had rather peeved him, to say the least. Still he would, no doubt, have found someone else to perform the job.

Included in our week's work was rest day, Friday, and as this was also the day we were paid, it necessitated us coming down to the shed, in our own time, to collect our wages. It was a common practice, for the foreman on duty at the time, to place a note on the check of the fireman who was required for a driving turn at midnight or soon after. When the man concerned received his cheque from the time clerk in charge, he would be given the note detailing him what time to book on. When this happened to me later on, when I became one of the senior hands and was first man available after midnight, I simply refused to accept the note and went on my way, leaving the foreman unaware that I was not coming at the time on the note. When this happened, the foreman on the midnight shift would be expecting me to come and, invariably, the job would be late in consequence. Needless to say, I was not popular with the Running Foreman, but I was sure in my mind that what I did was right; why should a man come to the shed in his own time and then be told something about work, all of which happened on what was supposed to be his rest day.

One day, when I arrived at the shed to take up my rostered work of firing, I was 'brought off' — a term used by locomotive men when they were taken off their regular routine to perform driving. The RSF advised me to walk to Warrington Station, to relieve a special parcels train and work it as far as Carnforth. My fireman was a mere youth of some seventeen summers, standing at a height of about 5ft.

The train, No. 6133, a tapered boiler 'Royal Scot', which was bound for Aberdeen, ran into Warrington with Rugby men on the footplate. I took a sly glance at my youthful stoker, and wondered how he was going to successfully place coal in the front corners of the 11ft. long firebox. While we were waiting for the station staff to complete the work of unloading and loading parcels, I had time to spread a good round of coal on the fire to give my little mate a flying start. At the same time I had the injector working to fill the boiler, ensuring that we would be in shipshape order before setting off with a heavy parcels train on the first twelve mile hop to Wigan.

Upon receiving the 'right away', I gently opened the regulator and the engine grudgingly began to move. With her 6ft. 9in. driving wheels she seemed reluctant to make her way out of the station but, after a furlong or so, she settled into her stride, and as she gained speed, the familiar one-two three, one-two-three rhythm of her three cylinders became distinct, with six exhaust beats blasting up the chimney with every revolution.

We rounded the curve at Dallam, doing considerably less than its 60m.p.h. speed restriction, but some three miles further, at Winwick Junction, we were approaching the maximum of 70m.p.h. controlling this point. My mate was now finding it difficult to keep his balance on the rocking footplate, for this type of locomotive was built with most of the weight 'on top' so to speak, the boiler being high due to the large wheels and the firebox slung over driving wheels, not bogies like the 'Duchess' class. Therefore, these engines rocked and rolled notoriously.

As we ran through the cutting towards Golborne, with the distant signal 'clear', I opened the firehole door and heaved a good fire into the box. I did this knowing that I had a clear road ahead, and could relax my vigilance for a few precious minutes while I fed the fire where my mate was falling short. This would suffice now, for I would be shutting off steam just after passing Bamfurlong, with the engine drifting the rest of the way into Wigan. This respite gave Alan, my fireman, time to bring her back to a reasonable working capacity again, filling her boiler and stoking the fire in readiness for the heavy haul up Boar's Head Bank. The 'Royal Scot' had to work hard and barked furiously from the front end, her exhaust belching sky-high as she laboured up that bank with her twenty laden parcel vans. As we topped the short summit of Coppul, I told Alan that from here onward it was all down bank, to Preston at least, and then we would be 'express' to Lancaster, a run of 23 miles over a fairly level road.

I felt slightly sorry for my mate, as he desperately tried to keep his feet on that unstable rocking footplate, and a couple of times he shot to the side of the cab but happily avoided hurting himself, as he grabbed hold of something solid to stop him being catapulted into the handbrake or the doors, both of which were made of good old-fashioned steel. The last lap, the remaining 6½ miles to Carnforth, was a comparatively easy run, and we were relieved on arrival at the platform by men from that depot, who told us to report to Control.

When we had eaten our sandwiches and drunk a cup of tea, I telephoned Control who told me to relieve the Carlisle to Willesden working, which would be arriving in about half an hour. This was rather a 'crack' train, as far as goods trains were concerned, being fully-fitted throughout. The engine was Camden-based 'Patriot' class No. 5550, referred to by the men as 'Baby Scots'. The driving wheels were of the same size as a 'Royal Scot' and the firebox, although still long, was not quite as long as those of her big sisters. Nevertheless, it took a considerable amount of skill to place coal in the front corners, and as firemen gained experience they became passed masters at 'hitting the ring', as it was called. To do this, the shovel would deflect itself off the firehole ring, as the man wielding it would deftly aim the blade right on to the very centre of the metal half-ring, on the bottom half of the firehole. The upper half was simply the deflector plate, which actually held the lower ring in position while at the same time, the ring also held the deflector plate in position. Anyone trying to fire a locomotive and not hitting the ring would find it tremendously exhausting, as he would have to lunge the coal with a mighty jerk and even then would not achieve the desired result.

The box of a 'Patriot' was long and sloping, and it took a great deal of ingenuity to stoke the fire in such a way as to have it thick under the door, sloping gradually down to a couple of inches at the front end, just like a wedge. Of course, my young mate lacked this experience, and I had to use the shovel frequently. I chose my opportunities, where possible waiting until sighting a distant signal then a long straight road before leaving the look-out and engaging in firing. This, of course, was particularly hazardous at night, with the glare of the flames dazzling one's vision when trying to see in the dark afterwards.

After leaving Carnforth, we had travelled only a short distance when we encountered the troughs. I manipulated the scoop, as Alan had not done it before, then we were headed for Lancaster with its stiff uphill gradient almost to Scotforth. The engine responded readily; this class was renowned for its hauling power, and would steam on bricks. The distant signal for Oubec was in the 'clear' and, when passing the box, the colour lights for Galgate and Bay Horse were green, so I bent down and walloped a fair quantity of fuel into the firebox.

When speeding through Scorton we passed over a bridge with a parapet, and as we flew by I thought I saw a glow on my side, somewhere near the intermediate driving wheel. I looked over the side, but could not see any cause for concern. The dusk of a late summer evening was creeping in from the Pennines, away to our left, while the sun, sinking into the Irish Sea to the west, cast long shadows and played slight tricks of illusion in the half light. Running over the little bridge spanning the Wyre, at Garstang, I saw a glow from the reflection of the parapet, and thought then that the ashpan was rather full. This did happen at times, when the 'firedroppers' did not clean the ashpan properly; the ashes in the pan, being high, would touch the bars and would eventually ignite, causing a fire in the ashpan. When this occurred the metal of the pan could, and often did, burn, thus causing a great deal of damage. Passing another parapet, at Barton & Broughton, I saw the glow again and decided to inspect my locomotive at Preston.

In those days, we hardly ever got a clear passage through Preston but tonight was the exception to the rule and, as we approached, the signals were in the 'clear' position. Well, it was getting late, and I wanted to have a couple of pints before the pubs shut. I kept going, expecting to be held at Standish, as was usual, but on approaching this junction, the signals were off for me to go through Wigan. Usually we were turned over the Whelley Line, in order to avoid Wigan, but we would not be long negotiating the long steep decline to Bamfurlong. It was uphill then to Golborne, and an easy run down through Winwick to Dallam where a set of men were waiting to relieve us.

I stopped outside the box, while the men walked across and climbed on to the footplate after we had climbed off. Walking past the driver's side of the the engine, so as not to be exposed to the fast line, I noticed the intermediate driving wheel. The boss on this type was hollow, and when I looked at it I could see for about a yard down the boss; the axlebox and journal were white hot, and the heat could be felt quite fiercely when standing about 3ft. from it. This, then, was the mysterious glow, so I shouted to the driver who had just relieved me not to start and to have a look at the trouble. It was obvious that the locomotive could not be worked forward, so it was arranged to place the train in the sidings and put the engine on the depot. Later, as I put away three lovely pints, I considered myself lucky to have escaped injury.

CHAPTER SIXTEEN

Taking a Fall

It was a bitterly cold, miserable, wet and dreary night in November. To make matters even worse, it was Saturday, and I had worked a train up to Edgeley where Leeds men had relieved us to work the train forward. Reporting to Control I was informed to walk to Cheadle Heath, to reman a mineral train from Buxton, so after a cup of tea I set off in that direction.

My fireman had not been in this area before, so I told him to follow me and, if I fell down a hole, not to fall in after me. This, of course, was supposed to be humourous, and not in the least to be taken literally. We left Edgeley and then proceeded along the road as far as the village, then made our way to the railroad, because there was no direct access to the place where we were to relieve our train.

In order to reach the railway, though, it was necessary to walk along a path marked 'Private', then along the banks of a pond which was home for a couple of pairs of swans. Often these hefty birds would resent our untimely trespass by swooping noisily across the water and scaring us out of our wits, especially at dead of night. Because of this, there were some of our drivers who would not venture that way for anything. We went this way tonight; not that we were brave, but simply because we did not know any other route. Creeping tentatively past, we succeeded in reaching the end of the path and then scrambled over the hedge to gain access to the railway, making our way towards Cheadle Village Junction where the line crossed the one coming from Buxton. Here we had to descend the banking, in order to reach the lower level. It was pitch dark, and precariously we groped along the uneven terrain knowing we could encounter sleepers and other material left here by platelayers for future replacement.

The next thing I knew I was falling . . . but into what? I was conscious of tall upright boards and, beyond them, the sky. My God! I thought, I am much too young to be snuffed out like a candle. Then it dawned on me; I was still falling. Suddenly I stopped falling, as I had hit the bottom. I think I clambered out of that hole a darn sight quicker than I had fallen into it, and when back on dry land I took stock of myself. The upper part of my body was dry, as were my feet and legs, but my middle was wet; all round the area of my posterior, my trousers, underpants and shirt were sopping wet through, while my outer garments were covered in clay. Still clutching the brew can in my hand, although quite unconsciously, I felt pain in my hand — the can must have swung round and hit the back of my hand, for there was a lump the size of a pigeon's egg where the rim at the bottom of the can had caught me. Apart from this there were no injuries, but I was freezing cold. The damp foggy night did nothing to help either, so I headed for the Heath to pick up my return train, hoping it would arrive early as I did not want to loiter about in my dilapidated condition.

When we reached Cheadle Heath we found our train had arrived, and waiting to travel home with us was a set of men from our own depot. Good! I thought, the driver can work the train back and let me travel in the brake van. When I suggested this, however, he did not seem at all in agreement so I told him not to bother; I would do my own job. Upon hearing my flippant retort he relented, and hesitantly offered to work in my stead. I then climbed into the brake van and proceeded to strip off my wet clothes, as far as decency would allow, and I placed them near the little stove; at least they would be a little drier on reaching Arpley.

Finishing in the very early hours of Sunday morning, I set forth on my weary way home. Clambering into bed next to my wife, who was cosily warm, she unconsciously moved to the other side of the bed muttering something about me 'being like a block of ice'. I smiled, and let her go back to sleep, knowing that it wasn't the right time to tell her of my unfortunate escapade.

CHAPTER SEVENTEEN

Pilot Duties

Booking on at 7.50a.m. one morning, for my own job of firing to Middlewich, the RSF told me to 'pilot' a Patricroft train to Crewe as the driver did not know the road. I felt disgusted; my own work was quite a pleasant day's task, running into the picturesque scenery of the lovely County of Cheshire.

I climbed on board to find an elderly driver from Patricroft, who made no attempt to vacate his corner in order to allow me to take over the manipulation of the locomotive. This, of course, he should have done; if he did not know the road he was strictly bound to hand over to the driver who was conducting him. Sometimes, however, when the man requiring the services of a pilot had a good idea of the route, he would politely ask if he could remain in charge. This request was usually granted, and it was an understood agreement that the driver who was piloting would point out any little matters of interest, as well as any other thing not quite known to the train driver.

All went well until we came to the Coalyard box, when the older driver almost shot out of the driving corner. Here we left the main line, and were turned down the road leading under a tunnel beneath Crewe Station, then on to the maze of metals which made up Crewe Sorting Sidings. It was obvious that this driver was lost here, and was only too willing to hand over the responsibility to someone else. If I had known this earlier, I would have ordered him out of the corner upon leaving Dallam. Despite everything, though, we carried on, later disposing of our train and then putting the engine on Crewe South Shed. The Patricroft men then made their way home, and I reported to the foreman at that depot, as was the practice.

I had now been on duty for just over an hour and was told to 'go and have a cup of tea', a polite way of telling me to go and sit in the messroom and await his pleasure. This I strongly detested, as very often the foreman on duty would clean forget all about a 'foreign' driver, and that poor unfortunate would sit there hour after hour twiddling his thumbs and staring into space. This, I'm afraid, was precisely what happened that morning; I was despatched to the land of the forgotten within the messroom. To sit there in a cabin, although not entirely strange, was certainly not 'my own' cabin at Dallam. The men in the cabin were, of course, mostly Crewe men and, although friendly, were not the same as men from our own depot. Here I sat watching the fingers on the clock creep laboriously round on leaden wheels, as hour after dreary hour ticked slowly by. There was no alternative because, if I went to the RSF and asked him if he wanted me for anything (meaning to work a train), he would probably say something like 'Oh, I

might need you for something!' After a dreary day spent sitting idly in a
cabin doing precisely nothing, I finally caught the 3.35p.m. train from
Crewe and landed at Dallam about 4.30p.m., making forty minutes overtime. This, then, was the undesirable aspect of 'piloting', as it meant being
with drivers from another depot instead of a mate of your own, and then
being stuck in a 'foreign' messroom for maybe hours on end. There was,
however, a job which was even worse; this was piloting, but with a veritable
difference.

On occasions, a tamping machine operator would require the services of a
locomotiveman to conduct him over certain roads. Of course, these men
knew little about signals although they were generally not interested, being
essentially permanent way workers. They were concerned with the railway
from another aspect, that being the state of the track, and it was their job to
see it was maintained in proper order. Due to Board of Trade regulations,
however, they were strictly bound to have a train driver with them to
monitor their movements. The locomotive driver was responsible for all
moves made by the machine regarding signals, dummys, and generally
working to the rule book.

The man driving the tamper would always be wearing ear-muffs, to protect him from the infernal row, so invariably the train driver left him to his
own resources, keeping within shouting distance in case he was required
when the machine was to pass signals. There was, of course, a snag —
where did the driver go? It was all right if there was a cabin nearby, but
usually the job was out in the country, and miles away from anywhere. If
there was a cabin nearby it could be used as a haven of shelter, but if, as was
often the case, no shelter was available, the driver simply sat upon the
grass if the weather was good and walked about if it was unkind.

Happily for locomotivemen, the men working the machines now know the
route they are working and, indeed, sign a route card the same as a train
driver, having been passed by a Footplate Inspector on the rule book. It
was certainly an unthankful job, but it counted towards those elusive turns
required to put a man on to his next rate of pay.

CHAPTER EIGHTEEN

A Difficult Trip

In answer to a knock on my door, early one Thursday morning, the call boy informed me to book on at 3.35a.m. for driving duties. Ah well, I thought, it's another turn, so I confirmed that I would be there. Arriving at the depot I found I was to work a special to Buxton, my fireman being a mere lad of sixteen years. Our engine was a Mogul, more commonly known as a 'Crab', and although they were not the best of engines they were strong, and capable of pulling tremendous loads. Eventually we backed up on Arpley Sidings, and set off on our way.

Things didn't go well right from the start, and while passing Lymm my mate told me the injector was not working properly. Going over to his side of the footplate, I juggled with the offending piece of mechanism until it 'sang', a term used when it was working correctly and not wasting water. I also noticed that the tender feed was leaking badly, and it would not be long before the tank needed filling at this rate. Grabbing the coal pick I gave the feed a terrific clout and, lo and behold, the water stopped trickling. So far, so good.

After a somewhat weary struggle we reached Chapel-en-le-Frith, and I had just stopped here, with the water-column opposite our tank, when the 'bobby' came running out of his box to inform me that there was a passenger train behind us, which we would delay if we took on water. Of course, I had to ignore his request to carry on, as our water was, by this time, rather low, and it would have been futile to proceed. The 'bobby' nearly had a fit, knowing that the passenger train would be stopped, but I told him to go back to his box and leave me to attend to my work. He went, muttering and no doubt cursing as well.

When climbing the very stiff gradient to Dove Holes the engine gave of her best, but as we had a heavy mineral train it was all she could do to keep her feet and pull it up this murderous incline. Reaching the box at Dove Holes, the 'bobby' there told us to 'back across the road' to let the passenger train go by (it was now waiting at Chapel-en-le-Frith), as our presence was stopping him from having a clear passage. To accomplish this move, we had to draw forward a train length until our engine was inside the mouth of the tunnel. We then had to look back, in order to see the guard's signal for us to set-back across the road, and peering through the smoke and fumes, I eventually took the brake off and let the train drag us back. At the same time I had to check her, as once the train got the better of the engine it would be impossible to stop, as there were no 'fitted' wagons attached. Even then, it was difficult to bring her to a stand when we were clear of the crossover.

A few minutes later the passenger train passed us, giving us a signal on his whistle which only locomotive men understand. This insult was for delaying him, and I smiled ironically; what else could I have done? I had a mammoth load with a run-down old 'Crab' that was heavy on water, and a young, inexperienced fireman. When he had gone by the points were turned for us, and the 'bobby' gave me the tip to proceed. This was easier said than done, as we now had to drag that heavy train over the bends of the cross-over and up that slippery incline. The engine strained to the utmost, and I dared not give her too much steam because one slip now and we were doomed. I opened the regulator precariously and, on the least sign of a slip, shut it again. Open ... shut ... open ... shut; so it went until my arms positively ached. It was no joke opening and shutting the regulator; one needed two hands normally but, when aching limbs were taxed to the utmost, a shoulder was employed to try to make the operation easier. After a titanic struggle we succeeded in reaching the mouth of the tunnel, but this is putting it mildly.

Entry into that infernal tunnel signalled the beginning of a nightmare, as it was two miles long and uphill all the way meaning that the engine had to be fired almost continually, and her boiler kept to a reasonable level. The fumes were choking and we could taste the sulphur, but we battled valiantly onwards. The absolute blackness of that underground road was heart-breaking and seemed to last an eternity, going on and on for ever. The engine was simply putting one side rod in front of the other and, in the dark subterranean world, it was as though she was actually walking. We plodded onward until, after what seemed like a lifetime, we saw a faint glimmer of dirty light which gradually widened into the shape of the tunnel end. At long last we crept into daylight, and I thanked my lucky stars that we had made it because, if anything had gone wrong inside that tunnel, it would have been unthinkable what we would have had to do in case of failure or accident. To come through on the footplate of an old engine was terrible in the extreme, but to walk back in the inky blackness, with absolutely no difference when one's eyes were open and when they were shut, would be enough to scare the wits out of the most lion-hearted.

Although we were out of the tunnel we still had to top the summit at Peak Forest but she trudged on her weary way, finally making it to the box at the top, 1,085ft. above sea level. We coasted down to the junction then, after rounding the corner following our passing through the shortest tunnel in England where, away to our left, was Blakeley Mill (the smallest station in England), we set off towards Topley Pike, uphill all the way on the last despairing lap to Buxton. We had been on duty now for some ten hours and had yet to reach home, although another driving turn was notched off the elusive 287.

CHAPTER NINETEEN

Flats, Springs and Bogies

One morning, having gone to bed expecting a good night's sleep, as my regular firing turn was at 2p.m. in the afternoon, my slumbers were rudely interrupted by that ogre in the shape of the knocker up, who informed me to book on at 4.13a.m. for the 4.58a.m. working to Rowsley. This was simply an empty wagon train, and who the genius was who decided that this train should run at such an ungodly time remains a mystery.

Our engine was a Class 8 freight, No. 8188, and was stationed at our own depot. Having prepared her for the road we set off for the sidings, to attach to the train of coal empties. After leaving the yard at Arpley we encountered the bank leading up to the bridge spanning the Manchester Ship Canal, a gradient of 1 in 135. This was not a particularly steep incline but, as we were climbing past the village of Latchford, I remarked to my fireman that they (we often referred to the train as 'they', meaning the wagons) were unusually heavy for empties. He agreed and we pressed on but, as we ran parallel to the main street leading from the village to the town, a man on a bicycle was gesticulating vigorously and pointing to our engine. We ignored him, and the incident was forgotten.

Some time later we stopped for signals at Cheadle and, in accordance with the rule book, my mate walked to the box to carry out Rule 55. On his way back he noticed something wrong with our bogies and, at his request, I alighted to examine them. I found that the spring of the nearside bogie had broken, and that the leaves had swung round and jammed into the spokes of the bogie thus preventing it from revolving. Using the services of a makeshift crowbar, in the shape of a shunting pole, we managed to dislodge the leaves when I moved the engine a couple of inches, and tied them out of harm's way with a piece of string from a sheet off a wagon. I then inspected the damage closer, to see if we could proceed. On top of the rim of the bogie was a small 'flat' but, about 6in. away from this, was another and far deeper 'flat'.

After pondering a little, I soon realised what had happened. We had come off the shed and run tender first to Walton Old Junction, after which we had run engine first the rest of the way here. The small 'flat' had been created on this short stretch, and the big one on the journey to Cheadle. This proved to me that the spring must have been broken when we left the shed, and I was responsible for the fit state of the locomotive having prepared it.

I informed the signalman that I would take the engine to the depot at Heaton Mersey, as it was not in a fit state to travel further. This we did, and returned home as passengers. Upon reaching Dallam Shed we went straight to the road on which the engine had stood, where we had prepared her some hours previously and, lo and behold, there in the pit were the rest of the leaves of the bogie spring. It did not take the work of an expert to dispose of them in a nearby ash wagon, to be dispatched out of sight and, we hoped, out of mind.

Upon reflection, later, I thought of the possible consequences had we been routed through Cheadle Village, as this would have necessitated taking the right-hand road at Northenden. As this was a junction with a speed restriction of 25m.p.h. to Cheadle Village, I hate to think how the engine would have reacted when taking a sharp curve with an immobile bogie!

Incidentally, the same luckless locomotive was involved in a sad accident some time later, when a burst steam-pipe occurred and made the engine bereft of brake power.

CHAPTER TWENTY

Passenger Stops

As men came to the age of retirement and left the service, other men would be promoted accordingly; the senior passed firemen became 'registered' drivers, and some men moved into higher links as seniority dictated. As this took place over the years, I became the 'oldest hand' passed fireman.

When manpower was strained, the senior passed man would be marked in place of a man who was sick, thus performing a whole week's driving. This was the situation when I was marked in place of a passenger link driver, and entailed working a motor train. I had passed for these jobs as a fireman, but had not been with an Inspector to act as a driver on this class of work. However, as five driving turns were involved, I decided to keep 'mum'.

I arrived at Arpley at 3.28a.m. Monday morning to prepare two engines and my own before turning off the shed to work the 6.15a.m. service to Ditton. Teddy, my fireman, was a quiet type with the unpretentious air of a farmer, and was a good honest worker. Therefore before starting on our journey we had a confab, as we would be running to Ditton motor first which was something I'd never done. There were five stations to call at, and I gained skill by practising stopping at these before running into Ditton, arriving there without incident. From here it was normal running, engine first, to Timperly, calling at all stations on the way. After detaching our human cargo, we ran empty stock to Broadheath where, once again, we became a passenger train. I would now be driving from the coach.

The first stop was Dunham Massey, and I reflected on the advice given to me the previous week by an 'old hand' driver — he warned me of the unpredictable characteristic of this village station. With this sound warning uppermost in my mind, I shut off steam in good time and let the train drift down the falling gradient. Braking early, I ran alongside the sleeper-built platform, and was just about to congratulate myself on my skill in stopping at the sloping end of the little station when, suddenly, it seemed as if a giant hand was shoving us through. Even though I was travelling at no more than a couple of miles an hour the train did not stop where I intended, and came to a halt with the window of my driving cab directly under the signal box.

The purpose of this box was to control the level crossing, and I reflected that it was lucky for me that the gates were in my favour; had they been set for the highway, I would have obviously demolished them. Before the 'bobby' could make any sarcastic remarks, however, I pointed to the foot of the box and shouted:

'That platform used to be here!'

Fuming with rage he slammed the window shut and, the next instant, we headed towards Heatley, and it was not long before we were coasting down the 1 in 135 gradient to Latchford. The wooden platform here was lined with office workers, the men having the uniform of the nine to five brigade of bowler hats, newspaper under the armpit and immaculately rolled brolly. It was amusing to see how they all stood in the very same spot every morning, patiently waiting like pawns on a chessboard.

I approached with the train under full control but suddenly, for no apparent reason, we came to an abrupt halt. This caused the people to rush to the south end of the platform, looking angrily at the driving compartment as they passed. Even when we arrived at the terminus they still glared as they went through the barrier. Climbing on to the engine I asked Teddy what went wrong at Latchford, and he smiled as he said he did not think I was going to stop. The smile vanished when I said that I blamed him; I did not tell him I was only joking. It was then that I told him to leave the brake alone on the following day, and he nodded agreement.

Next day, as we approached Latchford, and with the previous day's episode fresh in my mind, I seemed to allow for my mate's anxiety on the previous morning. Alas, in doing so I went sailing through the station, and finished up at the far end. Again the passengers had to charge along the uneven boards to reach our train, and if they were not pleased the day before, this morning they were furious.

Upon coming to a stand at Warrington they all turned deadly nightshade looks at me while one man, braver than the rest, came to my driving cab and, in the haughtiest of voices, apparently conjured up to make me feel inferior and said, quite firmly and deliberately:

'Driver! Yesterday you stopped at the far end of the station, this morning you stopped at this end; tomorrow, could we have 'middle for diddle'?

I looked him straight under the rim of his bowler and said:

'No!'

He was flabbergasted.

'Why ever not?' he exploded.

'I'm rest day tomorrow!'